Simran Bhui is a writer, creative facilitator, illustrator-in-the-making, child whisperer and a very clumsy human being. She was born in New Delhi, India, where she grew up with her parents and two siblings. Simran majored in English Literature, Mass Communication and Political Science, after which she did her post-graduation in Liberal Studies from Ashoka University. She has a certificate in Basics of Psychology and a diploma in TV Production and Screenwriting from Osmania University. Presently, she works as a research consultant at Mentora, the Institute for Life and Leadership.

Simran is fascinated by literary reimaginations, abstract thoughts, everyday polarities, mismatched clothes and every colour on the planet. Her organization, The Purple House, was created with the foremost intention of making people dip their fingers in paint, have heartfelt conversations with strangers and embrace their awkward selves with joy. She offers personal sessions and interactive workshops on topics like creativity, public speaking and stage fear. Simran is scared of spiders, doesn't understand math, swears by meditation, loves owls and can be reached at hello@simranbhui.com.

A Trickster's GUIDE to Happy LIVING

Simran Bhui

RUPA

Published by
Rupa Publications India Pvt. Ltd 2020
7/16, Ansari Road, Daryaganj
New Delhi 110002

Sales centres:
Allahabad Bengaluru Chennai
Hyderabad Jaipur Kathmandu
Kolkata Mumbai

Copyright © Simran Bhui 2020

ISBN: 978-93-5333-780-3

First impression 2020

10 9 8 7 6 5 4 3 2 1

The moral right of the author has been asserted.

Printed by Parksons Graphics Pvt. Ltd., Mumbai

To mom and dad.
You will always be home.

I heard happiness can be found in a place called Here.

Do you know how to get there?

CONTENTS

TRICKSTER
noun | trick·ster | \ ˈtrik-stər \
a playful, curious and crafty creator

NOTE FROM THE AUTHOR

All my life, I've wanted to be the girl with all the answers. All of them. It took me a while to realize how utterly boring that could get. So, in the last few years, I have been learning how to give that up. All I'd like to be now is the girl with the most questions.

Like… How can we live a greater life? How can we live without apology? With joy? Without judgement?

These questions have nudged and prodded me to do more. They have demanded that I step it up and choose more. Because you see, here's the thing about questions: They create room for wonder in your life.

They have made me write. And paint. Go on walks. Jump on dry leaves. Talk to people. Express gratitude. Be vulnerable. Play with kids. And puppies. Be messy. Heck, even awkward.

They have helped me find the fun amidst the chaos.

And right there, my lovely, is where I took my first step into the world of the curious and the wondering. That is where I began my journey of happy living.

Now, let me make something very clear to you: Happy living is not being happy all the time. It's a journey *to* happiness that begins when you start living in the question. It begins when you say 'yes'—yes, to adventures; yes, to curiosity; yes, to inspiration; yes, to vulnerability; yes, to life; and always, yes, to yourself.

This book is an invitation for you to do just that. It is a collection of tidbits, activities, musings, reflections, questions and borrowed epiphanies—all of which have steered my path along this journey. Let me warn you, though: This book has a mind of its own. As soon as you flip the page, I'm out. It's just the two of you then, off on an adventure of your own.

If that sounds like too big a commitment to make—I mean, come on, we *are* talking about *ten* whole weeks—by the words of a stranger you met on paper some three minutes ago, I get you. I really do. So maybe you don't take that leap just yet. Maybe, the only thing you begin to say yes to is to meet your co-pilot on this ride. You can figure the rest out later.

So, what say?

Would you like to play?

–S

'Here is where all the magic happens,' they say…

Hi there, Trickster.

Am I glad to see you! Welcome to a whole new conversation on happiness. For the next ten weeks, every day will be a chance for you to add something new to your life. All you need to do is be present. With me. And yourself. If you can, throw away your gadgets while we talk. Seriously. Toss them into the ocean. Or, if that sounds too extreme, bury them under a pillow fort. It will be fun to make. And you can even nap inside it later. Do what you must, but spend some time with me. The Internet will wait for you to get back, I promise.

You and I will get to spend a lot of quality time together for the next ten weeks. By the end of it, I'm going to know you a lot better than most peeps out there. But don't you worry; I'm very good at keeping things to myself, so all of your secrets will be safe with me.

I don't really have any secrets, so feel free to share everything I say with others… Okay, not everything. Just the things that make me sound cool. I have a rep to protect, too.

Here's how this arrangement will work: I am going to ask you to do something new every day. Now, I am not an expert on happiness; I'm just curious about it. So, I will have no answers for you. Just a whole bunch of questions. Each prompt that I offer will encourage you to write, reflect, sketch or get your hands dirty. At times, I may even ask you to do things you have never done before. Just work with me, okay? Joy is worth being vulnerable, so I'm guessing this will be worth your while, too.

How about you give me a name before we begin? Go ahead and do it. Just make sure it's absolutely bonkers. What's a road to happiness without some silliness on it, anyway?

What are you going to call me? _____.

Ha! That's cool. Let's just add 'zilla' at the end. I think 'zilla' makes everything sound cooler. Don't you?

Write it down again. With conviction. What are you going to call me? _____zilla.

Cool, even if I say so myself. And what am I calling you? _____. (Introduction Complete: 50 per cent)

That's a nice name. How old are you? _____.
(Introduction Complete: 50 per cent)

Caught ya!

That was a trick question, buddy. Age doesn't matter. Except when you have to drive. Or vote. Or fly a plane. Or be president. Or do a thousand different things, but my point is that it doesn't matter here. As far as I'm concerned, the only thing your age tells me is how many times you have revolved around the sun. Nothing else. I'm going to ask you to remember that, okay? There will be a pop-quiz later.

Final question: What are you expecting out of this journey? Write it down. For me and for yourself.

WHAT ARE MY EXPECTATIONS HERE?

1. _____

2. _____

3. _____

4. _____

I hear you.

Let's mark today's date, shall we? _____.
(Introduction Complete: 100 per cent)

Cool. Now let's begin…

Wait!

I almost forgot to tell you this. Remember: I am just a curious book. Nothing more. This journey will be what you make of it. No pressure, though.

Tighten your seatbelts.

Here we go…

HAPPINESS AND...
FEAR

Date: / /   **Week 1: Fear**

Hi there, Trickster.

I have a very important thing for you to do today. It's a bit ceremonial and I'm proud of myself for thinking of it. Do you remember that bit about saying yes that you began this journey with? I thought it was pretty cool. In fact, truth be told, I actually felt a little moved by it. Today is about that.

I have put together a Contract of Happy Living for you to sign. Like anything to do with happiness would, it has a lot of serious thought behind it. I wrote it. Well, most of it, anyway. There may be a few blank lines and clauses here and there. All that legal talk got me tired, okay? And there were some butterflies outside the window I was scheduled to chase. Really. You can even check my calendar after we are done here. Just take care of those gaps for me?

I want you to sign this contract and gift yourself the permission and commitment of saying yes to these ten weeks of playdates. Go on. Get to the page and sign it.

And remember: Do not break the contract, or else... Hmm. I can't think of a good threat right now. Can I tweet one to you later? Just don't break it in the meanwhile, okay?

CONTRACT OF HAPPY LIVING

I, _____, understand that I am embarking on a unique, vulnerable and adventurous journey of Happy Living and I choose to fully commit myself to this ride. I, _____, pledge to show up every day with a sense of play, curiosity and wonder. I commit to saying yes to the following:

1. Being open and non-judgemental

2. Encouraging my inner playmate

3. Asking tons of questions

4. And staying in the question

5. Stepping out of my comfort zone

6. _____

7. _____

I, _____, also commit to fully embracing this experience by offering my complete and undivided attention and participation. I, _____, pledge that I will not let anything or anyone (especially myself) hold me back from having as much fun as I can. I will be honest with myself, step up, welcome change and paint with my fingers when required to.

_____   _____
        (date)   (signature)

Yay! You did it.
    You are now bound by law and paper to obey everything I say.
        Just kiddin'. Have some water to celebrate this moment.
        Now get out of here. No! Don't peek at the next page.
        Go check your phone. I hear it buzzing under all of those pillows. Out!
        See you tomorrow.

Hi there, Trickster.

Welcome to Day 2.
    I have a very simple task for you to do today.
    Just draw me something. Nice. Or not nice. It's up to you.

Good job! That's a really good drawing. I'm going to hang it up in my room later. Can I ask you something before you leave, though? Did you draw inside that box? Why?

No, don't shake your head at me. All I asked was for you to draw me something. And then, I went ahead and put a big box in there because boxes are pretty and perfect and cool and why shouldn't I randomly put a box on a page if I feel like it?

I never asked you to draw inside the box though, bub. You did that all by yourself. You had all of that free space that you chose not to use. You assumed there was a limitation when there really wasn't. You stopped yourself from going big when there was no need to.

We all do that, don't we? We restrict ourselves. We find reasons to stay small. And sometimes, hidden. We think barriers into existence. And then, we learn to live with them.

Interesting, huh?

So, what do we do here now? Ask questions, my friend. Ask lots of questions. Stay in the question. You signed a contract about it, for cryin' out loud.

Look at some of the different parts of your life. The ones that aren't working. And the ones that are. And ask yourself: 'Is there something more that I can do here? Am I limiting myself in any way? What assumptions have I made? If I could do away with them, would I be able to live a happier life? A freer life?'

Stay in the question. And see what shows up.

Is there anything that you want to make note of here?

Cool. Now go draw outside the box, too.

I'll see you tomorrow.

P.S.: If you drew outside the box on the first try, kudos to you! I just really like making long speeches. Words are nice. Bye.

Hi there, Trickster.

That was a neat trick with the box last night, right? Today, I thought you and I could sit down and chat about limiting ourselves because of fears that aren't actually ours. Do you know what I'm talking about? Sometimes, we borrow fears from others because we think it's the only natural thing to do.

It's true! Let me tell you a story. I once met this girl who loved to talk. Even more than I did. She could talk for hours if no one interrupted her. But whenever anyone handed her a mic, all the words would just disappear from her brain. Poof! Gone. Just like that. Now the strange thing was that it had nothing to do with the crowd. Get rid of the mic and she would be fine. It didn't make any sense to her, so she just accepted it as one of her little quirks.

Then one day, someone asked her: 'When did you first decide you had to be afraid of the mic?' She looked at them like they were a fool. 'It's not something I decided,' she fumed. 'Humour me,' they pleaded.

So she rolled her eyes and started thinking about the first time she felt her throat close up in front of a microphone. It was when she was in the fifth grade, participating in a poetry recitation competition. A day before the contest, when she was in her room practising a piece by Robert Frost, her sister popped in to wish her luck. She gave her a big hug and said: 'Don't think too much, okay? It can be kinda scary when you have to speak through a mic. I have never been able to do it. My voice comes out all squeaky and my palms start sweating. It's horrible! Be prepared for it.'

Now this little girl, who didn't know any better, borrowed her sister's fear. Because she thought she had to. After all, it was only reasonable that she would feel the same things her sister had felt. Right? Now I don't know exactly how it happened, but somehow, she began thinking she had stage fright, too. And she lugged around that fear for years and years till the day that person helped her realize it wasn't hers to carry in the first place. Then, she neatly packaged it in a yellow cellophane sheet and sent it along its way.

Don't get me wrong, though. I'm not suggesting that it was a one-shot exercise. Of course, she spent time working on it afterwards. But the first step?

The realization that it was a fear she had borrowed from her sister years ago.

Which makes me wonder... How many such borrowed fears are you hauling around? Are they limiting the extent of joy you could feel in your life every day? Is it possible for you to let some of them go now?

Think about those times when you had the feeling of being sick to your stomach before you had to do something. Each time you felt your palms getting sweaty. Or your throat getting dry. Maybe it was before a math exam. A dentist's appointment. Before you had to dance in front of a crowd. Give a presentation. Say no. Talk to someone new. Say yes. Have a conversation with an authority figure. Speak up for yourself. Or go skydiving. Catch my drift?

Were any of those borrowed fears? What if they didn't really belong to you? Why don't you write some down?

HOW MANY FEARS HAVE I BORROWED FROM OTHERS?

1. _____

2. _____

3. _____

4. _____

Nice work, champ.

Can I tell you something else?

Almost all of your fears are borrowed. Or learned. There have been studies that prove this. All of us are born with two fears. Can you believe that? Only two! Do you know which ones? The fear of falling and the fear of loud sounds. Ha! We learn to be afraid of literally everything else.

Think about a few things that you're afraid of again. And ask yourself: 'Is there any value in me holding on to this fear?' The answer could be yes, sometimes. I mean, of course, there's merit in being afraid of touching a hot stove. Hurray for no burns! But in some cases, the answer could be no, too. Like, there may not be a lot of value in not using your voice. Or staying small.

Recognize which fears don't serve you anymore. Because acknowledgement is the first step to letting anything go. If that's what you choose, of course. The choice is yours, bud. It's always yours. More on this later.

That was a good speech, wasn't it?

I should be a speechwriter.

Somebody call the president.

See you tomorrow.

Hi there, Trickster.

I have something fun planned for you today. Pick up your pencil and eraser, because it's time to sketch again! Or if you're one of those really confident ones, then by all means, borrow my pen. Don't worry, though; I will not be drawing any trick boxes today.

We have talked a lot about this character called fear. But what does it even look like? Does it have a face? A nose? Some eyebrows? It's very important for us to know. How else are we going to put up those mugshots?

Can I go first? This is what fear looks like in my life. Yikes. Gives you the shivers, doesn't it?

Your turn now, bud. Go on and sketch me your fear. Show me what it looks like for you. Don't think about what this activity means. Just put your pen to paper and start sketching. Over to you.

Woo. Scary. You can head out now. I'll keep an eye out for it while you play. See you tomorrow.

Hi there, Trickster.

It's storytelling time! Have you ever used a post-it note? Isn't it amazing?

But did you know that its invention was a complete accident? Yes! Had it not been for some things that went horribly wrong, you and I would have been living in a world without any post-it notes. Yikes. Can you imagine how dull our study-tables would be?

Let me give you a quick run-through. A really smart person named Spencer Silver had some big plans. He was hard at work in his lab, looking for ways to develop an extraordinarily strong adhesive glue that could be used to build planes. Yes, the ones that actually fly. It was going to be some hardcore stuff, really.

The final product, though… Well, let's just say it was a little different from his expectations. What he ended up creating was this weak pressure-sensitive glue that gave away at the slightest pull. Hmm. Not very good for building planes, I guess.

He failed. And boy, did he fail spectacularly. But, out of that failure, came the post-it notes. How, you ask? Well, for starters, he refused to see his failure as the end of the road or as an anti-climactic conclusion to an exciting phase in his life. He saw it as an experiment. For six years, he stayed in the question. And then, another fellow called Arthur Fry came around with a bunch of ideas that ultimately gave us the post-it notes we adore so much.

Do you see where I'm going with this?

There's absolutely no point in being scared of failure. It doesn't help. Instead, stay curious. That's all. Failure is a conclusion, bud. When you stay out of the conclusion of not succeeding, you step into a world of greater possibilities. Of greater learning.

Now don't get me wrong here. I'm not suggesting that you also spend six years experimenting with something that didn't work the first time. Or the third. Or the thirtieth. Nope. That's not for me to tell you. Only you know if you have the time to do that. Or the will. Or the capacity. And it's okay to stop and rest if you don't. All I'm saying is: What if you stop labelling that entire experience in itself as a failure? What if you stop concluding that you weren't good enough to succeed? And begin to see failure as an interesting outcome, instead?

One that you can ask questions from.

One that you can have conversations with.

One that you can learn from.

That wouldn't be so bad now, would it?

Try it, bud. It will shift your perspective of failure. And change the way you approach it. Just try it. Once. Or thrice. For me?

Which brings us to today's task!

I'm going to give you three very interesting situations. And all you have to do is use your Trickster wand—your imagination—to find a way out of them.

Take a deep breath. Count till ten.

Ready? Go.

1. You have been invited for a talk at your school. The host calls out for you. The audience welcomes you with a thunderous applause. You take to the podium and neatly lay out the paper you're going to read from. Just then, a photographer angles her camera and clicks your picture with a blinding flash. You smile and look down at your paper. All you can see are some big black spots. You blink. Nothing. Your stomach flips. Your mind is blank. The audience is waiting. You have to say something. Now. What do you do?

2. You are participating in an innovation contest. For the better part of the summer, you spent your time developing the finest polaroid camera in the

world. The picture quality is the best anyone has ever seen, but the photos completely fade away after two weeks. Despite this very obvious flaw, your gut says that this is a worthwhile invention. You pack it up in a box, ready to present it the next day. What do you say?

3. You are at a… Actually, no. Enough of these hypothetical situations. You know the kind of stuff I'm talking about now. So, tell me about a similar incident from your life. Tell me about a situation where you came close to failing. Then, tell me how you turned it around. It could be something as simple as tripping on your laces while performing on stage. Or something a bit more complex, if you like. Over to you.
    What happened? What did you do? What did you learn?

Ha. This was fun, wasn't it? You are smarter than I thought you were.

And, hey… Now that you know failure is just a conclusion you can choose to step out of, here's a popular question by Robert Schuller for you: What would you attempt to do if you knew you would not fail?

No. Ssh. Don't start answering. Just stay with this for a while.

I sound so smart.

See you tomorrow.

Hi there, Trickster.

Can you believe Week 1 is almost over? Time really flies, huh?

I don't have anything fancy in mind for you today. Do you know what a permission slip is? I want you to write one for yourself.

Think of it as a Trickster's all-access hall pass. If you were the ultimate wish-granting authority of your life, what would you give yourself the permission to do? To live freely? Fiercely? And dare I say, happily?

When I wrote my first permission slip, I told myself that I'm allowed to live a happier life. I chose to stare fear in the face and do what I had to, anyway. I realized that it's okay to make mistakes and to not take myself that seriously all the time. I nudged myself to ask more questions and be more curious. To take up more space. And time. To show up. Use my voice. And be heard.

What about you, bub? Where's that pencil? What are you giving yourself permission to do? And be? What does your all-access hall pass say?

That sounds perfect. Hurray to granting permissions! I'll see you the day after.

HAPPINESS AND...
JUDGEMENTS

Date: / /

Hi there, Trickster.

Welcome to a whole new week! Of our playdates, I mean. Otherwise today might just be a Wednesday and you must think I'm some kind of weirdo who believes a new week starts on a Wednesday. We all know it starts on a Friday, right?

I'm kidding!

Wow. You were really judging me there for a second, weren't you? Admit it. We all do it. We all judge. Each other. Ourselves. All the damn time. It would be funny if it weren't so annoying. D'you get what I mean?

I used to judge myself a lot a few years ago. I'd look at some of the other books around me. And I would absolutely hate the fact that they knew more about the world than I did. All I wanted was to be as smart as they were. And I gave myself such a hard time when I couldn't.

Can I tell you something a nice lady once said to me about judgements?

She said that whenever she was judged as a child, it felt like someone was pushing her into a box she didn't want to get into, taping it up and throwing it into a dark corner of the room. Yikes. That really stuck with me. I guess that's what I felt like, too. Let me draw it for you so you can understand just how bad it was.

Yeah. All that darkness... Don't worry, though. I'm much better now. And anyway, I'm pretty smart too, right? RIGHT? Say yes! What in the world? I thought you and I were friends.

Ugh. Let's just move on to today's task.

You are going to need a pencil again, mate. No. Don't use a pen. Not even if you are really confident. Pens are very sharp. They hurt my skin. It's as thin as paper, you know?

HAHAHAHA! See what I did there? See? Pfft. And you thought I wasn't smart.

Anyway, I was wondering, if you had to give the term 'judgement' a physical shape and form, what would it be?

It's not fun to be judged. We all know that. Think about a time when you really wanted to do something and someone said that you couldn't. Maybe because they thought you weren't talented enough. Or tall enough. Or short enough. Or that there was no way in the world you could possibly learn German. You know what I'm talking about now, don't you?

Sketch me a judgement.

Think about all of those times when you were judged for being you. Think about how it made you feel. If you could give that experience a form, what would it be?

Hold on, buddy. What did I say? USE A PENCIL. Pens hurt.

I see what you mean. Can I give it a try, too?

Hm, I think this is what judgement looks like for me.

Do you know what that is? If you don't, go read *Harry Potter*. Right now. Out of my sight. I refuse to talk to you till you read all the books.

It's a dementor, buddy. Gives me the chills every single time.

Do you know how Queen Rowling described these creatures in *Harry Potter and the Prisoner of Azkaban*? She called them some of the foulest creatures that walk this earth. Let me read it out for you. Ahem. She said: 'They infest the darkest, filthiest places, they glory in decay and despair, they drain peace, hope and happiness out of the air around them… Get too near a dementor and every good feeling, every happy memory will be sucked out of you.'

Jeez. In the non-magical, non-Trickster world, I think that's what judgements do, too. They drain happiness and laughter out of the air. Poof! They make them disappear.

A Trickster knows that only happens if you let it, of course. But more on that later.

I'm loving your imagination, buddy. And hey? That lady who described the experience of being judged as being pushed into a box? She also told me what happened when she began to take care of herself. When she began to nourish her heart instead of the judgements.

Beautiful, ain't it? See you tomorrow.

Hi there, Trickster.

We covered a lot of ground yesterday, huh?

I'm having so much fun with you. Even though it took me some work to get you to see how smart I actually am. But it's all right. You'll learn with time.

Anyway, I'm very excited about today's prompt. Do you know why?

Stop guessing. You can't possibly know. Not unless you are a mind reader, in which case... Hey, can we talk after we're done here?

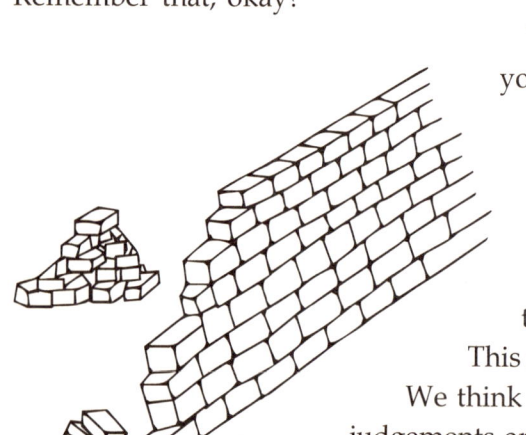

I'm excited because we get to open this big bag of tricks today! Yay! Say it with me. YAY!

Sorry, not sorry. I added three extra spoons of sugar to my milk this morning.

We could talk more. That's always an option with me. Or we could just get right down to it and see what the first trick in the bag is... Ready?

Ow, ow, ow. Finger cramp. Major finger cramp. There's no way I can finish this drawing. But hey, did you get it? You didn't get it, did you? DID YOU? Sigh.

It's a wall, mate! Sometimes the most obvious answer is the right one. Remember that, okay?

What's a wall got to do with judgements, you ask?

Turns out, a lot.

You see, we all build these walls around us. Brick by brick. We do it to protect ourselves. We mean for it to act as a barrier. Between us and all the bad opinions people may have of us. This is how we try to resist their judgements. We think that if we have a wall up, their darned judgements are never going to reach us. It's our way of saying: 'Hey, guess what, you rotten judgement flinger?

I don't care. Your judgements are your problems. Not mine. Here, take this!'

Get it now?

But the thing is… Having a wall up? It doesn't actually work all that well. In fact, I don't think it works at all. Because whenever we engage in an active pursuit to resist something, we spend a lot of our time focusing on it. We feed it our thoughts. And we feed it power. We use our energies to continuously push back against it. And that's more than enough for it to make us feel a certain way. And for us to lose our way on the road to happiness.

I mean, think about it—how in the world are you going to navigate with a wall around you? You could walk into a cactus and get your eyes poked. That would be nasty, wouldn't it?

We have another option here though, bud.

The Trickster's option.

Which is simple… Not to have a wall up at all!

Do you know what that does? It creates room for judgements in your life.

Sounds crazy? It is! But that doesn't mean it won't work.

You see, bud, when you put all of your walls down, you create more space around you. For judgements to fly through you. Past you. You make no attempts to hold on to them. Whether it is to embrace them or throw them back. You just let them pass by you. Without making them powerful. Or significant.

It's a much easier option.

And you know, it's pretty darn useless crouching behind a make-do wall, anyway. It doesn't keep the judgements out. It only keeps you in.

So, here's what you are going to do now. You are going to head on over to the page. You are going to pick up a pencil and sketch your barrier wall on it. And then when you finish drawing it, you are going to tear that page up. And say goodbye to your wall forever… Or, at least, for these ten weeks of playdates.

Ready? Let's go!

Now tear it up.
The same way that you built it.
Brick by brick.
At your own pace.
With deep breaths.
You got this.
I'm going to close my eyes so that this doesn't hurt.
See you tomorrow.

Hi there, Trickster.

Today, we are going to pull out another trick from the big bag of tricks. Are you ready to see it? Tada-a-a-a-a! Here it is…

Get it? Get it? No?

Oh, come on. I thought I nailed this one.

Well, those are a pair of glasses. You look through them. And you get to see a view. A *point* of view… A *different* point of view!

And that's how we arrive at our trick for today! Simple, innit? You just need to keep making associations. It helps build those creative muscles we will be flexing on this journey, okay?

This is a neat trick, bud. I've adopted it from something I heard the authors and speakers, Gary Douglas and Dain Heer, talk about on the Internet a few years ago. They called it 'interesting'. I call it 'different'. That's all.

Anyway, just think of it as something that disarms an incoming judgement. So, if you see a judgement rolling towards you at full speed…

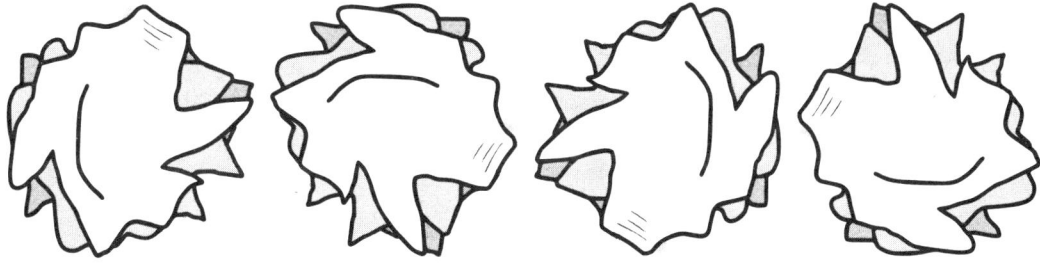

All you have to do is look at it and say: 'Hey, you, different point of view. What's up?'

And that's it. You have successfully used your Trickster wand to disarm that judgement and take away some of the power it could have had over you. You have snapped your fingers and eliminated any possibility of letting it get to you. I mean, you already have no barriers up. And now, you think that it's just someone's different point of view.

What can the judgement do now if you won't let it?

Nothing!

It's happy being a point of view.

Nice work, innit?

And it's so wonderfully simple, too.

Do you know why this works, bud?

Because a point of view only becomes a judgement when you agree with it or resist it. When you do neither, it has no significance in your life. All it gets to be is someone's random point of view at a random point in time. And why should that hold any power over you?

Isn't that cool?

So, let's do something now, okay? Let's dust our pants and disarm some judgements.

Make me a list. Write down some of the judgements that have come along your way in the past: Did they stop you from walking further ahead on the road to happiness? What if they were just some different points of view?

It could be when someone said that you were a little too short to play basketball. Or when they concluded that you can't sing. Or dance. Or do math. Or be an astrophysicist. Or that red doesn't look good on you. Or that you should smile more often. Or... Hm... Let me think... Maybe when someone thought you were 'too much': Too loud, too present, too fat, too thin, too confident, too... I don't know. It could be anything, buddy.

Just make sure to include actual judgements though, all right? Not gentle, meaningful feedback. D'you know the difference between the two? Whether or not they were meant to be kind. Judgements aren't purposed to build you up. Meaningful feedback is.

You know the kind of stuff I'm talking about now. And even if you don't, you at least have a vague idea about it. So go on now. Make me a list.

HOW MANY DIFFERENT POINTS OF VIEW HAVE LIMITED ME IN THE PAST?

1. _____

2. _____

3. _____

4. _____

Good job, champ! That's one heck of a list.

Now go back to it. Look at each point again and say: 'Hi, you different point of view. I have held on to you for long enough. You can go now, okay?'

Do it. Even if it feels silly.

And hey, why don't you try this the next time you are in a conversation with someone, too? If you sense a judgement approaching you, just think: 'Oh, there's a different point of view right there!' Chances are, you will no longer feel the need to react to what they are saying.

You will still say whatever you have to, of course. But when you do, you will not have lost control. You will not have reacted. You will have chosen to act, instead. And if no one has ever said this to you before: Happiness is the sum of your actions.

Stay with this before you go to bed, all right?

Psst: If you think this trick isn't working, then just stick your tongue out at the people who judge you. That'll show them. Just don't quote me on this, okay?

I'll see you tomorrow.

Hi there, Trickster.

Is it a good day today? Take me out sometime, won't you? It's been a while since I have been outdoors. And who knows what a walk might add to your life? If nothing else, we could sit under some trees and look at the squirrels! Or crunch some dry leaves with our fingers. Doesn't that sound amazing?

Anyhoo, I really liked that list you made last night. Did it change the way you thought of those judgements at all? If not, go back again and ask: 'You are all just a bunch of different and interesting points of view, aren't you?' Try it. They might say yes.

Speaking of, I was thinking about a similar list you made last week. Your list of borrowed fears, remember? And I couldn't help but wonder if this trick would work there, too. I mean, isn't everything in life some kind of a point of view, anyway?

So, consider this: What if some of your fears were just someone else's points of view that you made significant somewhere along the way? And what if you could disarm those fears just like you disarm judgements? How would that change things? Would it help bring more joy into your life?

I wonder…

Let's try it? Together. What do you say?

Let's make another list. Jot down some fears that you can think of. Look at them and say: 'Oh, hi. I see you now. I see that you are just a point of view.

Gosh, you have been one all along, haven't you? Go on, now. It's time for you to leave.'

See if it works. And if it does, do you realize what a big game changer that would be? The next time that little voice in your head whispers 'I'm scared of…,' you could just respond with: 'Huh, what a different point of view for me to have here.' And then, who knows? It might just leave you with more room to choose bravery instead of fear.

Go on, now. Pick up your pencil. And make me that list.

HOW MANY OF MY FEARS ARE JUST DIFFERENT POINTS OF VIEW?

1._____

2._____

3._____

4._____

There you go. It really is that simple, bud.

Can I say something else before you leave?

I mean, both of us know that I'm going to, but still. It's polite to ask.

Sometimes we don't trust the simpler things in life to work, because how can they? Our problems are so complex. Their solutions must be complex too, right? Wrong. Not always.

The most tricky problems often have the simplest solutions. We just need to be willing to trust them. Even if they seem ridiculously, a-second-grader-could-do-this simple.

You don't have to take my word for it.

Just try it for yourself. And let me know how it goes, okay?

See you tomorrow.

Hi there, Trickster.

Ya-a-a-a-a-awn.

Why did you wake me up? I was having such happy dreams.

Oh. The prompt. Right.

Let's do this quickly so I can go back to sleep, all right?

Okay so, here's the thing: I find it incredibly funny that you humans have built entire cultures, systems and structures around judgement. No, really. You have.

Think of any social media platform. Take your pick. I can't name any here or I might get into trouble. And I definitely don't want to go through that again.

All of your popular social media platforms are built to invite judgements. You like something. Dislike something else. Some things make you laugh. Others make you angry. Some might even make you say, 'Wow!' And then there are those very special ones that you heart.

I tried it once—this social media thing. I put up a very funny status with my picture. Do you know how many likes I got? NONE. Even after thirty whole minutes! I was so disappointed that I took it off. I wanted all of those likes and hearts and wows and ha-has. And it felt very bad when I got none. Know what I mean?

That constant careful calculation you do before you put something up? The right filters, the funny captions, the popular hashtags… All because you want to be judged positively? Because you want to get as many people to like what you have posted as you can? And at any cost, you want to steer clear of what I went through?

Well, of course, y'all are going to be worrying about being judged all the time in real life, too! That's what these platforms do.

Now I'm not going to ask you to just stop using these apps. That's unrealistic. And let's be honest, you find all the funny cat pictures on these platforms, so clearly, they have their benefits, too. I'm just asking you to be aware. Be aware of where you are doing things just to get likes. And where you are stopping yourself from saying something because you think you won't get any. That's all. That's not so bad now, is it?

I know I can't ask you to do this on your actual social media handles, but hey, do something here. Write me a status update that you did not put up online because it wasn't cool enough to get you likes. It could be a lame joke. Or an emotional anecdote. Both of which are very cool according to me, by the way. Just take to the page and jot down something you weren't able to put up online.

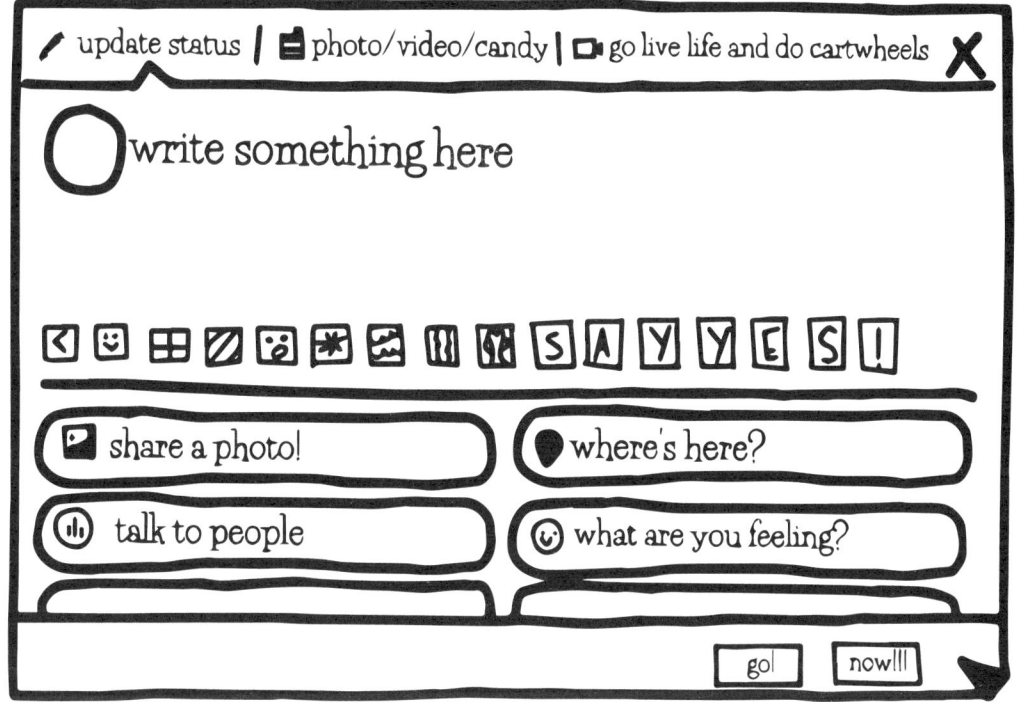

Ha! That was very nice. Here. You can have a 'like' from me.

What the heck. Take a heart too.

And now if you just go away and let me sleep, I'll throw a 'ha-ha' and 'wow' into the mix. Deal?

Off you go now. Goodnight, buddy. See you tomorrow.

Hi there, Trickster.

I have a question for you today. After these last two weeks of talking about fears and judgements, just answer this: Have you spoken up in front of people lately? Voluntarily?

If you have, cheers! Have an oreo chocolate and banana milkshake and tell me how it felt. Careful! It's spilling.

And if you haven't, then that's okay, too. Just tell me why, bud. What's stopping you? Is it fear or excitement? What do you think?

That wasn't a stupid question. I promise. Turns out, fear and excitement feel very similar in the body. And guess what? They even release the same chemicals in the brain! I mean, think about it. Your stomach flips. Your skin tingles. Your heart races. You feel a little lightheaded. Somewhat on edge. Similar, aren't they? Ha! So couldn't it be possible, then, for us to misidentify our excitement as fear from time to time?

And hey, maybe this can be another trick for your toolbox, too. Every time you feel scared of doing something, ask yourself this. Close your eyes. Breathe. Be open to change. And ask: 'Is this fear or excitement? Anxiety or anticipation?'

Try to change the way you think about those feelings in your body. Rephrase that entire experience as excitement. And replace the negative statements in your head with some questions.

Which brings me to my next point: Is there anything else that has stopped you from speaking up voluntarily in front of people? What conclusions have you made that are stopping you? Why don't you make a note of them here?

1. _____

2. _____

3. _____

4. _____

5. _____

There you go.

The answer was in the question, buddy. The answer is *always* in the question.

You have made some conclusions about what's going to happen if you speak up. These are the negative statements I was talking about. You know what they do, these conclusions? They lock you up. They make you small. And they leave you with no room for new possibilities. Or happiness. That doesn't sound very nice now, does it?

Stay curious, my friend. Ask questions. Ask yourself lots and lots of questions. Go wild with them. Ask: 'What is really happening here? Am I limiting myself in any way? Am I afraid of being judged? Is this fear mine? Heck, is this even fear?'

Choose your combination of questions and then disarm them. Say: 'Wow. So many different points of view! What will speaking up actually feel like? And what can I do to enjoy the experience as much as I can?' Then, go ahead and do it. Grab the mic. Even if it is to say: 'Hi! I just want to hear what my voice sounds like. Huh. Not so squeaky, after all.'

Sounds good?

And this is just an example, pal. You can use this everywhere if you wish. You can use it every time something stops you on your journey of happy living.

Now, can you do one last thing for me before you leave? Think of three things that you're afraid of doing. Write down a conclusion or negative statement about each of them. Then, replace every one of these statements with a question, just like we did a minute ago.

Ready? Over to you.

NEGATIVE STATEMENTS	HAPPY QUESTIONS
1.	1.
2.	2.
3.	3.

Look at that. I'm so proud of you, bud. Keep on keepin' on.

See you the day after.

HAPPINESS AND...
THE INNER CRITIC

Date: / /

Hi there, Trickster.

It's so good to see you. I may have missed you yesterday. Just a teensy bit. But we don't have time to talk about that right now. We need to get straight down to business. This is serious. And important. It's seriously important.

Do you know who your inner critic is?

Yes? No? Maybe?

It's that voice inside your head that censors everything you think and say. Many times, it even stops you from doing what you want to do. Your inner critic says toxic stuff like: 'Ugh. You call *that* trying?', 'You think *that* is a reason to be happy?' or 'Seriously, what's wrong with you?'

Yikes! Horrible, ain't it? If you ask me, it's one of the biggest obstacles on the road to happy living. And today, it's time for us to give that darned voice a face.

Can I go first? I promise I'll be quick.

This is what my inner critic looks like.

Na-uh. Don't let it fool you. It looks harmless. But that's just for show. Trust me. I can hear it shouting inside my head right now. It's very unhappy with the fact that I caught it in the act. And, it doesn't like that I'm talking about it out loud to you.

My inner critic has stopped me from doing so much, bud. It has stopped me from saying so much. It has erased so many of my words long before they had a chance to come out into the world. It has pushed me to create limitations in my life. To make assumptions. It has stopped me from trying. From believing. And I might as well admit it now, from truly living.

And today, it has a face.

Do you know why that's important? Because now I can look at it for what it truly is. A nasty little character who doesn't know how to let anyone around it be happy. It's miserable all the darned time. And you know what? I've had enough of its misery.

This is why I keep asking you to draw these things, bud. 'Cause once we give them a face—something to associate them with—we begin to wriggle out of the control and power that they have had over us. They are no longer some faceless all-powerful, all-consuming masters of darkness that we must bow down to. Nope. They are just some unpleasant characters. They have a face. And we can cut 'em out of our lives, whenever we wish to. Makes sense?

Now pick up your pencil, sharpen it and sketch me your inner critic. And as soon as I know what this character looks like for you, I'm going to stand outside the door while you create joy and make sure it has a hard time finding a place to park at in your life, okay?

Come on, now. Take to the page and tell me.

What does that nasty voice in your head look like?

Got it. Good. That's all for today. Go play. I'm guarding the door.

See you tomorrow.

Hi there, Trickster.

You did a very good job last night. And don't worry, okay? I'm still on the lookout for your inner critic. I will body block it if I have to, but it's not coming anywhere near you. Not on my turf. Not on my watch.

But, like, say if I fall asleep and it sneaks past me and taps you on your shoulder, do me a solid? Keep moving forward, anyway? Shrug your shoulders and let it rattle on. You just keep on walking, all right? Don't stop. Never stop.

Is that a deal?

Good. I'm glad we reached that agreement.

Now what do you say we move on to what we are here to do today?

It's quite simple, really. All I want you to do is to list me some of your 'I ams' and 'I am nots'. That's all.

We all have that list, don't we? Don't you?

Do you think you're too old to learn a new language? There you go! That's your first 'I am...' right there. Do you think you are not meant to learn Salsa dancing? That's one 'I am not...' We aren't looking for anything other than the everyday here, pal. We are looking at all the different ways in which our inner critic defines and labels us each morning.

We are looking at the 'I am too old to...' or 'I am too young to...'

We are looking at the 'I am too talented to...' or 'I am too unskilled to...'

We are even looking at the 'I am too good looking to...' or 'I am not good enough to...'

Get what I mean?

I'll be honest: I think I'm too old to learn German and be a self-taught language book. I also think I'm too young to be a history book. There are days when I think I'm a lot of fun, so I don't let myself be sad in front of anyone. And I believe with every page that binds me together that I'm too funny to be an encyclopaedia. But let me tell you a secret? I also think I'm not smart enough to be one. And on and on and on... Trust me, this list doesn't end.

Now, these definitions? They are the limitations our inner critic creates around us. And today, we are going to hold up our flashlights, dust around our heads and examine them. Closely.

Take a moment and be honest with me, bud. Be honest with yourself. Do you have a similar list of labels for yourself? Are they a set of conclusions that you are buying into? Have you subscribed to the limitations that your inner critic has created for you?

Well, it's time to click the unsubscribe button, 'cause there's so much more to you than those labels. And tell you what? Beneath all the conclusions, definitions and judgements of who you are and who you are not, there's a sleeping giant waiting to be stirred awake.

No, no. Don't be afraid of it. It's a good giant. Of possibilities. Of choices. Of free will. So pick up a stick and poke the giant, boo. But first, list me some labels, won't you? Hop on over to the page and draw yourself lots of circles. And then, fill each circle with some of your 'I ams' and 'I am nots'. GOOOO!

There you go. So many labels. So many definitions. So many conclusions.

Let me ask you something, though: Who are you really? Who would you like to be?

No. Ssh. Don't answer that. Not yet. I don't need one. And you don't, either. It's just a question. Let's not turn it into an answer so soon. Okay?

Remember to ask yourself this every morning. I'm going to go make my list now.

See you tomorrow, okay?

Hi there, Trickster.

It's so good to see you!

You and I spoke a lot about labels yesterday. We listed some, too. It was fun. But we have only just scratched the surface, bud. You see, I spent a lot of time thinking after you left last night. And I wondered why we even allow our inner critics to define us with these labels. I mean, yeah, I get that this is what we are taught to do in this world, but there has to be something more to it than just that, right?

What is the value of labelling ourselves with these 'I ams' and 'I am nots'? There has to be *some* value. Or we wouldn't do it.

So you know what I did? I looked at my own list. And I asked myself: 'What is the value of me holding on to this label, this particular point of view?' And y'know what I think? For starters, I think it lets me off the hook. For a lot of things. Like for not trying. I'm too old for this; what's the point in trying now, anyway? And if I do try, it lets me off the hook for failing. I can just shrug my shoulders and say: 'Oh, you know how it is at my age. I already knew I wouldn't be able to learn a new language. I only gave it a shot for fun. And I just wanted to learn the bad words, anyway. Wanna hear some?'

Get it?

When I think I'm too funny to be an encyclopaedia, it gives me an excuse to not try to be smarter. And when I think I'm too fun to ask my friends for emotional support, it gives me an excuse to not be vulnerable and get in touch with what I'm feeling. And sometimes, that's a lot more comfortable than the alternative. Do you see where I'm going with this?

What is the value of holding on to your list of labels? What has been the value all along? How does it serve you? What is its purpose in your life? Why don't you write down what you think? Ready? Let's go!

Psst: Don't you love it when I sound so serious and smart? I do. It tells me that I can have a deeper side, too. Huh. There's more to me than I thought, I guess. Let me ponder over that while you make your list.

WHAT IS THE VALUE OF HOLDING ON TO MY LABELS?

1._____

2._____

3._____

4._____

There you go.

Now you can see both sides of the coin. You know how your labels limit you. And you know how they serve you, too. Even if it is in some twisted way that you couldn't have thought of earlier. Even if it is to let you off the hook in front of people. Or yourself. Heck, maybe some of these labels protect you, too.

The choice is yours now, bud.

You get to choose whether you want to carry any of these labels around with you.

Me? I'm choosing to let go of mine. Why? Because I think life will be more fun if I do. I could learn a new language. And fail. Try again. Fail better. Or succeed. And it wouldn't matter either way. Because the only 'I am...' I'm going to carry around with myself is this: I am curious. That's all. That's really all. And I mean, isn't it nice to pack light, anyway?

Whatever you choose, pal, I'm going to cheer for you. There's no right or wrong answer here. And you can always choose again. You can choose every morning. Every twenty-two and a half seconds. What are you choosing right now, though?

Yay! Cheers! Celebrations!

Now get out of here and go roll around in some confetti.

See you tomorrow.

Hi there, Trickster.

I have someone I'd like to introduce you to today. Do you think we can do that? Yes?

Don't get too excited, though. No. Put those flowers away. And stop boiling water for tea! Stop. Listen to me. I don't like this character very much, okay? And I don't want to pretend like I do, either. Well, not anymore, at least. So no, we don't have to fluff the cushions. And we definitely don't have to serve it the good chocolate. Let's save that for later, all right?

Sigh. Let me back up a little and tell you how it all began. It walked into my life very early on. While I was still quite young. And it told me its name was Perfectionism. Boy, did that sound fancy. I couldn't believe it wanted to be *my* friend. D'you know that feeling?

It made me so many promises. It told me that it would always look after me. And it would make sure that everything I put out in the world would be perfect. That my work and reputation would glisten with sparkly drops of crystal-clear flawlessness. Its words, not mine! All of that sounded very tempting. And I fell for it.

I thought I could count on it. I thought it had my best interests at heart And I would tell anyone who would half listen the importance it held in my life. Dang it, I think I even put it on my resume once. Can you believe that?

Ugh. It was all a sham, buddy. ALL OF IT. Do you know how it ensured that everything I did was perfect? By never letting me do anything! It scared me. Mocked me. And became best friends with my inner critic. It constantly judged me. And it reduced me to a single conclusion: 'You are not good enough for this yet.'

It had a very sly way of doing it though, so it took me a while to realize what it was up to. Once, I wanted to learn how to dance. And I talked to it about joining a dance class. It smiled sweetly, held my hand and said: 'Well, of course you must join a dance class, my friend!' Pause. 'But only after you learn how to dance well.'

It was unwilling to let me do things poorly. So you know what? I never did anything at all. I never tried any of the things I thought would make me happy and bring me joy. Then one day, I picked up a set of cleaning solution and wiped my glasses clean. Hmm. Could've framed that sentence a whole lot better, but you get what I mean, don't you? I was talking to a friend and they told me how the author Elizabeth Gilbert talks about perfectionism in her book, *Big Magic: Creative Living Beyond Fear*. That conversation made me look at it for what it really was. And I dropped my water and gasped with shock.

Do you want to know what I saw? What perfectionism looked like?

Brace yourself. Here goes…

Recognize it? It was fear in a fancy hat! That's what perfectionism is, bud. That's what it always is. It's 'fear in fancy shoes and a mink coat, pretending to be elegant when actually it's just terrified.' Yikes! But do you realize what a big revelation this is?

Perfectionism is just your fear getting smart. That's all it ever is. Perfectionism is always fear in disguise. It's a state of judgement . It feigns elegance. It pretends to add some value to your life. Don't let it fool you, though. Because the only thing that perfectionism ever tells you is that you aren't good enough to do anything. Heck, to even try.

So, yep, now you see why I don't like it very much. In fact, truth be told, I don't like it at all. And I hope you won't, either.

Can you do something for me now? Remember that sketch you made of your fear in the first week? Draw it again. And give it a nice hat, some slick shoes, a rad tattoo or whatever else you think it puts on whenever it's in disguise. Okay?

Yeah, that's what perfectionism looks like in your life, bud.

Now answer me this: What has perfectionism stopped you from doing? Is there something that you would love to do so much that it makes you unwilling to do it poorly? Or at all? Where in your life are you waiting to learn how to dance well before you join a dance class? Where in your life are you waiting to write a *New York Times* bestselling book before you ever even pick up a pen? Where in your life are you waiting to play like Tendulkar before you ever borrow your sibling's bat? What have you been refusing to do because you fear you won't be good enough? How has all of that limited the amount of joy you could add to your life right away?

WHERE HAS PERFECTIONISM IN A STUPID HAT STOPPED ME?

1. _____

2. _____

3. _____

4. _____

Aye, aye, aye. I get you. I really do. And I'm glad you see perfectionism for what it really is now. Fear thought it was smart. Well, turns out we're smarter. Why don't you go celebrate this moment now? Maybe with some candy?

See you tomorrow.

Hi there, Trickster.

How's it going?

My head is still spinning from all the candy we had last night. So I really can't talk much right now. I must spin. Spin, spin, spin. Ha! Don't you just love a good sugar rush?

You know what? I say we continue celebrating today. What do you think, huh? Let's kick back and have some old-fashioned, colourful pun.

HAHAHAHAHAHA. Get it? Get it? Man, I'm so funny.

Pick up some crayons or paints bud, 'cause you're about to get a-creating. Today, we are going to stare perfectionism in the face and choose happiness instead of fear. We are going to create something stupid. We are going to create it terribly. And you know what? We are going to have a lot of fun doing it, too.

Ha! Take that, perfectionism, you stupid thing.

Let's not talk any more, okay? Let's not even think. For the next forty-five seconds, let your mind be blank. And just take to the page and do anything that might be fun for you. That might bring a hint of a smile to your face. You could write me the worst poem that has ever been written. Or you could paint me the worst painting you can possibly make.

Do whatever. Just be absolutely terrible. Be unbelievably terrible. And have fun with it. Have I said that enough? Ready to get started? Take over the page. Assume that it's empty. Go!

OMG! THAT LOOKED LIKE IT WAS SO MUCH FUN!

Now imagine if every day could be like this. If it could be about finding the joy of being instead of the judgement of doing. Happy, happy? We're getting there, bud. Slowly. Surely. Now go show that to everyone you know. EVERYONE! Oooh, I think I still have some candy left in the back. See you tomorrow.

Hi there, Trickster.

I have been waiting for you to get here. With excitement.

Today is going to be something different, I reckon. I love using words like reckon, by the way. I think they make me sound smart.

Anyhoo... Can I talk to you about a poem today?

It's this wonderful piece called *Bluebird* by Charles Bukowski. There are many layers to it, but let's save them for later. Let me just tell you what he writes about in the poem, okay?

Bukowski talks about a bluebird that lives inside his heart. Think of that little bird as his gentle, passionate and vulnerable self, which he hides from everyone in the world. All the time. It wants to step out. It wants to chirp in the open. But Bukowski doesn't let it. Why? 'Cause he fears it will mess him up. It will change the way people see him. And respond to him. So, he asks it to stay down. Out of sight. In his heart. Hidden.

But sometimes, when everyone's asleep at night, he quietly — cautiously — lets the bird out. He lets it taste freedom. He lets it sing. And play. He lets it know that he knows it exists. That he's thinking about it, too. In the quiet of the night, when no one can see it and no one can hear it, Bukowski's bluebird has a voice. Till the sun rises in the morning again, his bluebird is allowed to sing.

Sigh. I love that poem. Very much. If you can, go read it once we are done here.

It always makes me think. Especially when Bukowski says that he makes sure no one ever knows it exists. I wonder: Where is my bluebird? Am I hiding it too? Because of what others might have to say about the songs it sings? Because of what I may have to say about it?

Eh. I don't know, pal. I really don't.

But I do know what I would like to do now. I would like to keep it perched on my head for everyone in the world to see. For everyone to hear. Heck, for me to hear. I would like it to keep singing in the glory of the morning sun and in the quiet of the evening moon. I would like it to be untamed. And free. Bold. Fierce. Wild. And flawed.

Do you want to say hi to my bluebird? Will you sing it a song? Look!

Sigh. It's my precious. Why don't you show me what your bluebird looks like now? And after you're done, maybe you could cut it out and keep it somewhere near you? To always remind you to let it sing. Regardless of what your inner critic says. And to remind you to sing along, too. Even if it's on an off-key note. Okay? Lalalalala. Always. Come on! Sketch.

Beauts! Now cut it out, all right?

I'm going to do a little cheer for our bluebirds.

See you the day after.

HAPPINESS AND...
EMOTIONS

(PART ONE)

Date: / /

Hi there, Trickster.

Welcome back and come on in, already!

We have arrived at a very important juncture in our journey together, pal. Today we are going to sit down and start thinking and talking about ourselves, our feelings, our emotions and... EXCUSE ME! WILL YOU STOP YAWNING, PLEASE?

Gosh! Come on. Give me a chance, at least? This isn't going to be much of a drag. I promise. In fact, I'm even willing to make a deal with you: I'll scratch out the thinking part altogether, if you agree to do some of the talking. Cool?

So now, the only thing you have to do this week is... To just do it. Talk. Don't think about it. Don't analyse anything. Don't calculate your answers. Just say the first thing that comes to your mind. Got it?

Trust. Trust that you are allowed to talk about your feelings. Trust that you know what you are doing here. Trust that you can't get this wrong. Just trust.

And I'm going to ask you to be honest here too, bud.

With me. And with yourself. Especially with yourself, okay?

Let's begin. Do you know what ANTs are? We are going to start this week by picking up a big hammer and squashing the living daylights out of them.

You think I'm kidding, but I'm not. Look.

Whoa. Easy there, Thor. Keep that down. Just for a moment. You'll get to swing it around in a minute. Let's just chat for a bit first.

So, these ANTs… What? No, of course I'm not talking about some harmless creatures carrying tiny grains of sugar around! How could you even… Do you think I'm some kind of a monster? COME ON.

I'm talking about a different kind of ANT: Automatic Negative Thoughts.

That just became a lot less terrifying, didn't it?

Hmm, let's see. Can I read out how someone much smarter than me describes them? Ahem. Dr Daniel Amen says that Automatic Negative Thoughts are 'cynical, gloomy, and complaining thoughts that just seem to keep coming all by themselves.' Yikes.

Think of them as these nasty little characters that start crawling around in your head, randomly rattling on about whatever is going on in your life and convincing you that nothing is going to turn out all right. Absolutely nothing.

Delightful, aren't they?

ANTs give us anxiety. They feed on our happiness. Heck, they even receive marching orders from our inner critics every morning. And they lead us into an entire spiral of self-doubt and negative thinking.

So what do we do with them, then?

The same thing we have been doing all along, buddy. The same thing we did with our fears, judgements and critics.

We picture them. Give them a face. Wriggle out of their control. We recognize where they exist. What their voice sounds like. What their habits are. Where they eat. And then, we slowly start getting rid of them. At our own pace. We start saying no. We refuse to give them any power. We choose to forgive ourselves for having given them power in the past. And for when we may give them power again in the future. And then, we choose to nourish ourselves, not the ANTs. Every single day. That's how we become Tricksters.

Cool? Cool.

Ugh. Look at 'em all smug.

Now, before we do anything else, we need to know where they have been living. We need to locate them. In our thoughts. Our actions. Sometimes, even our behaviours. We may discover that most of them huddle around one corner, but let's still look everywhere, yeah? We don't want to miss the rogue ones, after all.

Let's go!

Pick up a pencil and make me a list, mate.

Tell me where these ANTs are living. Where they have been ruling.

Talk to me about those situations in your life where your head is often clouded with negative, complaining thoughts. It could be when you think one bad score on a science exam means that you will have to repeat the entire school year. When you believe that it's either all or nothing. If it ain't always, it's gotta be never.

Talk to me about those situations where you tend to focus only on the downside. Like when someone has eighteen good things to say about you, but you only care about the two that aren't that nice.

You could mention the times where you lean towards predicting the worst possible outcome. When you are convinced that something bad will definitely happen. Or when you believe that you always know what the other person is thinking about you. And those thoughts sure aren't pretty. Look at where you use labels to limit yourself. Look at where you blame others. Look at where you beat yourself up with guilt for no good reason.

It could be when you think you aren't good enough. Or that everyone in the room is laughing at the pimple on your forehead. Or whispering about how you've made your hair. Or how you speak. Or that your group for a big project blames only you for a bad review. Or that the professors taking the viva are going to fail you because they didn't smile. Not even once.

D'you see what I mean now?

These are all situations where you may have all kinds of Automatic Negative Thoughts crawling around in your head. Telling you that things will go wrong. Because they always go wrong. Convincing you that you are no good. Rattling on and on and on. Discounting you. Attacking your self-esteem. Putting you on edge. Complaining about everything. Without evidence. Always without evidence.

Do you think you can list me some of your ANTs now?

Jot down the first few things that you can come up with. Come on. I'm listening.

UGH, WOULD YOU LOOK AT THESE HORRIBLE ANTS?

1. _____

2. _____

3. _____

4. _____

Ah. I hear you, buddy. I hear you. Great job.

Now, look at that list again. These are your ANTs. These situations are where they are living. Feasting on your happiness. Dancing around in circles. And probably welcoming new ANT-babies, too. And you know what? Just by telling yourself about them, you have already picked up that big hammer to chase 'em out.

Just don't think of the ant squashing as me promoting actual violence though, okay? What I'm saying here is this: Now that you are aware of these thoughts, monitor them. Keep your eyes open. Look around. Perk up your ears. Listen. And whenever you hear them or see them crawling around, show them the back door. Firmly. And peacefully. Okay?

One last thing? Remember: Don't believe everything you think.

No, I didn't say it. I mean, I wish I did, but I didn't. Allan Lokos, the author of *Pocket Peace: Effective Practices for Enlightened Living,* did. And he's pretty smart and wonderful, isn't he?

Maybe you could write that down? And put it up somewhere?

Out you go now. Time to look for a post-it note.

See you tomorrow.

Hi there, Trickster.

How's it going today?

We spent quite some time talking about ANTs last night. We picked up our magnifiers and looked at where they have been hiding. Where they have been thriving. Then, as kindly and firmly as we could, we held open the back door and showed them the way out of our lives. Powerful stuff, wasn't it?

Now from what I've heard, these creatures have a way of sneaking back into our lives when they think we aren't looking. Irritatingly crafty, aren't they?

Well, I wasn't just going to stand around and look while they schemed and plotted and built hidden tunnels to our thoughts again now, was I? So you know what I did? I looked for other ways to get rid of them. To scare them off. I called up friends and wrote long emails to kind strangers I found on the Internet. I even searched for hashtags on Twitter. And then, I found a very cool trick to send those pesky little ANTs running away from our lives for good measure.

D'ya know what the trick is called?

Affirmations.

Sigh. Such a beautiful word, innit?

An affirmation is a thought, a belief and a promise. It is when curiosity and wonder are packaged together in a sentence. Affirmations are very powerful antidotes to Automatic Negative Thoughts. They push our brains to form new clusters of Positive Energising Thoughts (PETs). And I mean, let's admit it: PETs over ANTs any day, right?

Now this is where it gets good. You can use an affirmation whenever you see an ANT crawling around in your thoughts. You can even use them to talk over your ANTs. To shut them up whenever they are trying to discount you. And to send them running off in the opposite direction for good measure. Actually, you know what? Just think of affirmations as these big, happy scarecrows for your ANTs.

But that's not all. You can use affirmations daily, too. Every morning. Every night. You can write them down on small pieces of paper and stick them up in places you look at very often. So that you can keep on saying them to yourself a few times a day.

And yeah, I get that it sounds embarrassing, bud. I get that it can be.

But listen, who cares? Who's looking? Who knows? No one!

And no one has to, either.

You don't have to do this in front of people. And you don't have to tell anyone about it either. You are allowed to do things just for yourself. Things that are meant only for you. To be kind to yourself. To have fun. And maybe, to experiment a little as well.

And come on, I bet you do all kinds of embarrassing things whenever you are alone, anyway. I mean, your pyjama dance routine isn't exactly stuff for *So You Think You Can Dance*, right? So, why not do this too? Why not spend a few minutes each day to be kind to yourself?

How often do we do that? And what would change if we did?

…Have you come around or do I need to say more things?

Yay! I knew you would agree.

Now, a word of caution: When you use affirmations, you may feel like your inner critic is shuffling around, trying very hard to listen in on what you are saying. It's threatened by positive self-talk, so don't be surprised if it says all kinds of mean things to stop you.

Ignore it. Let it rattle on, if it must. Or write down the stuff it's saying. Become aware of its voice. Do whatever floats your boat, but keep on using your affirmations every day. Or at least till the end of our time together, okay?

Are you ready to give this a shot?

Hm, let me think. You can't go wrong with this. Look at yesterday's list. Those are some areas of your life where you don't feel that good about yourself. Think about what each ANT is saying to you there. And counter it with a positive energising thought, instead.

So, say an ANT makes you believe this: 'I can't possibly speak in front of an audience. I'll forget my speech, my voice will crack, everyone will laugh and I'll run away crying.' Eugh. Try countering it. Say: 'I can enjoy sharing my ideas, I can connect with an audience and words can come naturally to me.' Or make it into a question! That's even better. Ask: 'What steps can I take to speak effortlessly on stage?'

Fill your affirmations with curiosity. And positivity. And love. And all the good energies of the world. Don't use words like not, no, can't, don't, won't, shan't... You get the drill, don't you? Try it, bud. Just try it.

Oh, and you can make some general everyday affirmations, too! Like for when you get up in the morning. You could ask: 'What grand adventures wait for me today?' Or, 'Today, I am confident and comfortable with myself.' Or... 'I deserve happiness.' Or, let me think... Maybe this: 'I am willing to experience my creative potential.' And: 'Today, I choose bravery.'

Get it? Think of this as a way of emotionally supporting yourself on this journey. And if a particular affirmation doesn't work for you, if it fills you with dread instead of hope, then change it. Rewrite it. Make it open-ended. Have fun with it.

Are we on the same page now? Good.

So go on, now. Write down some happy affirmations for yourself. Commencing #MissionDefeatTheANTs in 3... 2... 1... Go!

COME HERE AND LOOK AT THESE COOL AFFIRMATIONS!

1. _____

2. _____

3. _____

4. _____

What a list, bud. What a list.

Ha! Would you look at that?

The ANTs are already running away.

Why don't you go read it again? And again? And again?

I'll see you tomorrow.

Hi there, Trickster.

I have been thinking all day about what we can do on our playdate today. And I think I've come up with something fun. And simple. Maybe even meaningful.

Yesterday, we sat together and wrote down some affirmations. So that we could learn how to be kind to ourselves, emotionally support ourselves and be our own cheerleaders with some fancy pom-poms.

But can we be honest with each other for a moment here, please?

Can we admit that there are times when we don't think we can do it? Heck, when we don't even want to do it? Lift ourselves up, cheer ourselves on, say all sorts of nice things to our reflection in the mirror... Any of it. D'you get what I'm saying? Sometimes we don't think we have it in us to be there for ourselves.

What do we do then?

Do we let the ANTs declare victory?

Do we let our inner critics build a fort of self-doubt in our minds?

HECK, NO. No, no, no. We alert the village and call in the troops. Do you know what that means? It means that we choose to reach out to those who care for us. We choose to let them in. We choose to accept help. And ask for it. Always ask for it.

We all need a tribe, pal. All of us do. We need a tribe of family, friends and professionals that we can count on. That we can trust. That we can talk to. A tribe of people who want the best for us. Who are there for us.

Do you already have names popping up in your head? Of people you can trust yourself with? Good. I'm going to ask you to write down their names. Along with their phone numbers, birthdays, email addresses and Instagram handles. Whatever you want. Whatever you need to remind yourself of their presence in your life. To remind yourself to reach out to them when you need to. To never shy away from asking them to step in and take care of you. Support you. Cheer you on. Listen to you. Sit in silence with you. Offer you random motivational speeches. Maybe even some candy. And love. Lots of love. And hugs. Or fist bumps, if that's what you prefer.

Wait! One last thing: When I made this list for the first time, I wrote my goldfish's name on it. Like, thrice. So don't worry if you want to repeat the same name again and again, okay?

Over to you...

HEY, WOULD YOU LOOK AT MY COOL TRIBE?

favourite human

parent(s)

comfortable with silence

a grandparent (or more)

coolest sibling or cousin

knows it all

doesn't know anything, but what the heck?

brings the best food

has the friendliest puppy

will dance it out

Now go throw some flowers at them as a way of saying thank you. Go, go, go! I'll see you tomorrow.

Hi there, Trickster.

You're finally here!

Listen, I have been meaning to ask you something since we spoke last night. Did you get a chance to thank your tribe for being your tribe? Even if it was only in your head? Even if it was only a fleeting moment of being truly grateful? Yes? No? Maybe?

We are on a unique, unique journey, pal. We are here to get a taste of what it means to be a Trickster living the good life. Living curiously. Living creatively. Living courageously.

But there's something we need to talk about that is essential for us to move forward on this journey. Something that's essential to any Trickster's journey. Are you ready to hear it?

Bring on the drum rolls!

Woot, woot!

Why doesn't life come with background music all the time? And who do I write to about this?

Ok, ok, I'll come back to the point.

That something else? It's gratitude!

STOP ROLLING YOUR EYES AT ONCE.

Oof. Why are you making me yell so much this week?

Gratitude isn't just a cheesy word for the books, pal. It's not just a brief feeling we experience a moment before drinking hot cocoa. It's so much more than that. So. Much. More.

Gratitude is a state of being. It's a way of life.

An invitation to experience everything around you a little bit more fully.

Think of it as a muscle. That all Tricksters flex daily. Without fail.

Do you know why gratitude is such a powerful trick for your toolbox, mate? Because it makes you step out of conclusions. And definitions.

It reminds you of all the possibilities that surround you.

It reminds you of goodness.

And light.

Love.

And puppies.

I don't know, okay? It always reminds me of puppies.

Gratitude is a trick that you can use every single day as a positive energising thought.

To create more.

To get rid of your ANTs.

To think outside the box.

To get off the hamster wheel of self-pity.

To laugh a little more.

Or to simply remember that there's more to your life than meets the eye.

And if none of this is good enough for you, then how about this?

To sleep a little better at night.

Ha. HA! I knew that would catch your attention. I just knew it. I love that I can speak your language now.

Are you finally onboard with this trick now? GOOD.

Gosh. The things I have to say…

But here's the thing: It's just so easy to forget to be grateful sometimes. I mean, let's be honest? There's so much happening around us all the darned time that it's only natural for it to skip our minds sometimes, right? RIGHT?

Well, get ready to soak in my brilliance 'cause I found a great way for you to remember!

You are going to find yourself a gratitude rock. Right freakin' now.

Get out of your house. And go for a walk. Jump on any dry leaves you see on the way. That's crucial. You must hear them crunch. Keep an eye out for a small rock. Or a pebble. If you already have one in your house, that'll work too. Look for something that easily fits in the palm of your hand. You want to be able to really hold it. Curl your fingers around it. Look for one that feels good.

You'll know when you see it.

It will stand out to you.

Once you find your rock, keep it somewhere you will see daily. Maybe by your bedside? Or on your study table? In your pocket?

Now every day before you go to sleep, just hold it tightly and think about one thing that you are grateful for. Just one. Think about it. And let a sense of gratitude settle in and stay with you for a few seconds. Really reel it in. Take your time with it. Let it fill you up. Completely. And then say the words thank you. Actually say them.

And that's it. REALLY. That's all you need to do to flex this muscle. That's all you need to do to actively make some space for gratitude in your life.

It's that simple.

The rock is important because it serves as a physical reminder.

Think of it as a cue.

And well, also because: Gratitude rocks! HAHAHA. Get it? GET IT?

No? Whatever.

Get out and find yourself that rock now.

NOW.

I'll see you tomorrow.

Hi there, Trickster.

Tell me: Did you find your gratitude rock yet? Hm?

If you haven't, go find it right now. Go. Get out of here. I'll wait.

If you have… Well, then a big yay for you! YAY! I wonder what your life is going to look like with a healthy dose of gratitude in it now.

But you know what? I get that there might be a few days here and there when you might not be able to think of things to be grateful for. Mind you, I'm not saying that you will run out of stuff. 'Cause more often than not, there's at least one or two things to be thankful for, right? Even if it's just nutella. Or a hot walnut brownie. Or mint chocolate chip ice cream. Yum. Or…

Wait, what were we talking about again?

Oh, right. All I'm saying is that we all have those days sometimes when we find it a little hard to see the sunny side of things, you know?

Today is for days like those.

I want you to close your eyes for a minute. And think of the best things that have ever happened to you. Think of the times you laughed so hard that your tummy started to ache. And the water you were drinking started to come out of your nose. Think of when you felt safe. Protected. And warm. Think of the times you ate so much candy that you went on a crazy sugar rush. And danced till your feet began to hurt. Think of when you experienced an overwhelming amount of love. Think of the times when you ate entire tubs of ice cream. And your nose became numb from all the cold. Think of when you felt an engulfing sense of satisfaction. A pause. Contentment. Think of the times you shared a secret and received only acceptance. Think of when a puppy licked your face. Think of the best moments of your life.

Sigh. Happy, happy?

And is that a smile I see?

Now I want you to preserve all of these memories in a big jar. So that if a day ever comes when all you can feel is cold dread, you can open the jar and relive these happy memories… And maybe, just maybe, warm yourself up again. Okay?

Look at the jar I made for you. Fill it up with as many memories as you can. And if you run out of space… Congratulations! It's a great thing. Just draw more jars. Draw as many of them as you like. Fit them in the margins, if you must.

And if you can't fill it up completely, then congratulations, too! Honestly. Because life's greatest moments are on their way. Brace yourself. And just come back to this page and fill it up as you go.

Wow. How did you get so lucky?

Close the lid real tight and come back to this page whenever you need to, all right?

And, hey… Did you enjoy doing this? Even a little bit? Then what do you think about including a memory jar in your life this year? Wait! Don't run away. Hear me out. It's really simple. All you have to do is keep one big mason jar somewhere in your room. And whenever something good happens, just jot it down on a post-it note and slip it inside the jar. You can even throw in photos, trinkets, movie stubs, train tickets… Whatever brings you joy. And at the end of the year, you will have one big serving of happiness inside the jar, just waiting for you to dig in.

Doesn't that sound positively spectacular?

Think about it.

Now go and make some more happy memories today.

I'll see you tomorrow.

Hi there, Trickster.

Gosh! What a month, amirite?

Can you believe that we've been at this for only four weeks now? Ha! Me neither! I mean, we have done so much. We have talked so much. And... Huh? What's that?

Sigh. FINE. *I* have talked so much. Happy?

But, hey... We've both come so far, haven't we?

I think today is a good time for us to sit down and have a little chat about surrender.

You see, I know surrender all too well.

I have worked with the idea of it for the better part of my life.

And I have struggled with it for the better part of my life, too. I don't quite know how to explain it bud, except that... Whenever I used to create or do anything, I went through all of these different emotional states. It started with hope. Then I felt dread. Thrill. Anxiety. Joy. Uncertainty. Confidence. Stress. Ecstasy.

It all came and went.

It was like I was a boat.

And there were waves all around me.

Which took me up and down. High and low.

Those waves? Creation.

Or so I thought.

It was only when I learned how to surrender that I realized creation wasn't those waves.

Creation was the wind pushing the boat forward.

That's all it ever did. That's all it ever wanted to do. Push me forward. Lead me closer to my North. Each day. Every day.

The waves? It was just me getting in

my own way. It was when I paused to ask perfectionism for permission to create. And when I gave fear a seat on the voting table. It was when I wanted each sentence to be just right before I even uttered a single word. And when I constantly worried about what others would think of my work.

I let myself become this self-important, self-censored creator.

And I got in my own way.

D'you know what creation did all this while, bud? It shook its head and calmly waited for me to come back to it so that we could go on wild and vulnerable adventures together. Move forward. Have lots of fun. Eat candy. And play with confetti.

So many of us do that, don't we? We get in our own way. We end up tripping ourselves. Over and over and over again.

D'you know the best way to deal with this?

You guessed it!

Surrender.

Resign.

To your senses. To your curiosity. To what brings you wonder and joy.

Relinquish control. Give in to what your curiosity is telling you. And create your life. Create not for anything or anyone. Create for the sake of it. Create for the joy of it. Surrender. And just create.

So, this is where we are right now: I want you to pick up your pencil and write yourself a resignation letter. Resign from this job of a self-important, self-censored creator. It doesn't matter if you think of yourself as a creative person or not. That's just a definition. Resign so that you can stop labelling yourself. So that you can stop employing fear and perfectionism to trip you over on our journey. So that you can go on wild adventures with your curiosity and creativity. So that you can breathe easy. Be more free. And happier. A little more vulnerable. Maybe even flawed. Resign so that the wind can take you where it must.

Go on. Address the letter to yourself. And resign.

Psst: Maybe you can also resign from the job of having to make sure this letter sounds like it was written by Shakespeare on a good day. Stop editing your thoughts, mate. Remember: An imperfect page is better than a blank page. Just write.

Ha! Turn around and feel the wind, bud.
    You are one step closer to flying.
    See you tomorrow.
    Oops! I mean the day after.

HAPPINESS AND...
EMOTIONS

(PART TWO)

Week 5: Emotions II

Hi there, Trickster.

I have something unique in mind for us today.

We ended the last week by writing ourselves a resignation letter. By surrendering. We moved a few steps closer to being wild and free Tricksters. But let's just put everything out in the open today, all right? Surrendering takes practice, too!

I mean, yeah, writing that letter was a powerful first step, but there's more to it than just that. It takes practice to get out of our heads. Out of our way. Out of the page. Know what I mean? We have been wired to think and act in a certain way for so long that it's only natural for us to fight the act of surrendering.

And we might as well admit it: Control is comfortable.

Even if it doesn't work. It's still comfortable.

Surrendering is scary, isn't it?

So today, I'd like for us to practise moving that muscle a little.

Listen closely. Here's what you are going to do: You are going to sketch something in total darkness. Complete, absolute, I-am-going-to-trip-over-my-own-feet-and-break-my-nose darkness. You can either switch off all the lights or just close your eyes. Whatever floats your boat. Heck, you can even blindfold yourself if you like a little drama.

Sketch me something in total darkness.

Play with lines. And shapes. And patterns. Dang it, throw in some colours if you want.

Give up control. Let your hands move on their own. Then switch on the lights. Or open your eyes. And be prepared to be surprised by what you see.

Ready?

Ohmigosh, I'm so excited!

Start from wherever you'd like.

GOOOOO!

OMG SO MUCH FUN. SO. MUCH. FUN.

See! Surrendering doesn't *have* to be scary.

Can I go try it now, too?

Byeeee.

See you tomorrow.

Hi there, Trickster.

Did you know that blankness is a trigger for happiness, too?
    Perhaps, one of the greater ones.
    So there you have it. Some blankness.
    Remember: Curiosity trumps control.
    Now do something with it. Or don't.

There we go. That was interesting, wasn't it?
    See you tomorrow.

Hi there, Trickster.

I hope you got some exercise last night 'cause we are about to do some lifting.

No, it's not negotiable.

Yes, you may have a chocolate oreo shake after we are done.

Can we move on now?

So, here's the thing: I've been thinking about all that we have been creating for ourselves in the past month. We have been creating more gratitude. Some wild, free and vulnerable adventures. More curiosity. Songs of bluebirds. More courage. And freedom.

And I wonder: How much space do we need to create for all that we have entering into our lives right now? D'you see where I'm going with this?

Stretch out those muscles and pick up a shovel, bud. It's time to do some decluttering.

Now, I understand how collecting stuff can be fun sometimes. I even have a shoebox full of ticket stubs to prove it to you. I mean, come on, was I seriously going to throw away my admission pass to Disneyland? Heck, no. That's where I met Simba!

But we're talking about a different kind of decluttering today, pal: Emotional decluttering. We are talking about all the thoughts, feelings, labels and emotions that you have been lugging around... For no good reason, really. We are talking about the kind of stuff that holds you back. Or reins you in.

Can I let you in on a secret, pal?

Tricksters always travel light. They don't pack a lot of stuff to carry around. Think about it: How are they going to do cartwheels along the road with a heavy bag hanging around their necks? It might get stuck on a lamppost. And they might hit their heads on a nail. Or, I don't know, break their arms or something. It's just easier to pack light.

So, why don't you spend a few minutes to think about everything that you are ready to release from your life right now? It could be some emotions that no longer serve you. Or some grudges that have overstayed their welcome. I mean, it's probably best to forget about that one time that kid in fourth grade bought the last cup of chocolate ice cream before you could, right? Hm... What else? It could be some conclusions that have limited you. Some judgements. Memories. Regrets. Labels. Catch my drift? Think about all of the old, broken, torn and worn out stuff that has been hoarding your mental space.

What can you let go of now to create more room for joy in your life?

More room for wonder?

More room for yourself?

Do you have a few things in mind? Think of them. Dig them up. Tie them around some helium balloons. Say your goodbyes. Shed a tear. Or laugh. And then let go and ask them to leave. For good, okay?

Here, let me start you off with a few balloons.

I love how this is going.

Have you run out of space? You already know what to do. Just draw yourself some more balloons. Draw as many as you need, okay?

I'm going to leave you to it.

See you tomorrow.

Hi there, Trickster.

Something happened after you left last night.

I decided to do some decluttering of my own. So, I called some friends, bought some balloons, wrote down my list and got ready to let go. It would have gone brilliantly. Except that one balloon's string got caught under my shoe. I immediately tried to pull it free so that it could float away with all of its other balloon friends, but I think I must have pulled too hard. Because I fell. No joke. I fell flat on my face.

Ugh. I think I bruised something. Ow. A lot of things.

But well, at least the balloon flew away, right?

Anyway. I was so annoyed. I wanted to scream. Very loudly. But I was outside. On the roof. All of my friends were there. They were looking. And so, I didn't.

You know how it is sometimes, right? You can't always scream in a public place. Even if there are things that are really bothering you at the time.

But… You can scream here. In front of me. No one else is here. Only you. And me. So, let's do this, yeah?

Think of everything that is bothering you right now. Everything that's making you feel angry. Or irritated. Or stressed out. It could even be the stuff I keep asking you to do each day. I mean, I will frown if you scream about that, but I won't hold it against you. Which is my way of saying: I'm still going to ask you to keep doing these things! Ha.

Do you have a few things in mind right now?

Good. Write down everything you have thought of on this page.

Write them huge. Maybe even in caps.

Write them as if you are screaming. Write them in no particular order.

And stare at them for twenty seconds. Ok? Go!

Now simply turn the page.

Maybe glue these sheets together if you feel like it.

And leave. Go on. There's nothing else left for you to do here now.

I'll see you tomorrow.

Hi there, Trickster.

That sure was a whole lot of screaming you did last night.

My ears are still ringing. Lalalalalala. So much ringing.

But, listen, tell me something: How did it feel? Wasn't it kind of nice to just write down everything that was bothering you at the moment? To have it get out of your head and onto the page? To give it some space in a book rather than a corner of your head? Heck, to actually acknowledge it rather than keep ignoring it? Hm?

Well, guess what? That's exactly what we are here to do today, too.

We are here to… Wait, what are you doing?

Stop stuffing cotton in your ears! There won't be any yelling today. YES, I PROMISE. Oh. Oops. Ahem… I mean, yes, I promise. Hee-hee.

So, as I was saying, we are here to name our emotions today, bud. That's all. That doesn't sound like it's going to get very loud now, does it? See? I'm an *excellent* promise-keeper. Aren't I? AREN'T I?

Dang it. Fell right into that one… Whatever. Let's just move on, all right?

Here's what I want you to do: Think of something that's driving you up the wall today. Something that's making your fingers tingle with raw emotion. With anger. Or frustration. Or anxiety. Or any one of the thousand different things that you can possibly feel.

It could be the traffic that's out on the roads today. Or it could be how slow the Internet is. Or the fact that you didn't get any sleep last night. Even though you were in bed by eleven. It could be that one person who keeps judging you. And the clothes you wear. The work you do. It could even be a conversation that you had with a friend. Where they said something you didn't like very much. Like how pictures of cats playing with yarns are overrated. I mean, how dare they? It could be anything, really.

Stop and notice the emotion that's causing you to feel that way. Instead of gulping down your feelings, actually acknowledge them. Look towards the emotion that's demanding your attention. And call it out. Ask: 'Anger, old friend, is this you?'

And voila! That's enough for it to stop throwing a big ol' tantrum in your head. Even if it is only for a moment. That's enough for it to take a few steps back. And create some room for you to step in, instead. For you to call the shots. Not the emotion. Know what I mean?

D'you know why this trick is so powerful, mate?

Because it's so simple! It's so ridiculously simple. And you remember what we said about simple solutions, right? They work! Like magic. They don't take time. You can use them whenever you want. Wherever you want. Even if you are around people. Isn't that amazing?

So, what do you say we give it a shot right now?

Make me a list of the three things that are bothering you the most right now. And think about what they're making you feel. Notice the one emotion that's dominating your experience of each of these situations. And give those emotions names. Call 'em out. Sketch small faces next to them if you want. Just tell them that you see them. And ask them to take a few steps back. Firmly. Ready? Over to you…

HMMM, SO THIS IS WHAT I'M REALLY FEELING, HUH?

1._____

_____

2._____

_____

3._____

_____

Huh. Would you look at that?

Looks like someone's been paying close attention to what they're feeling.

Can I just say something else before you leave, bud? You don't *have* to act on an emotion just because you are aware of it. And you don't have to not act on an emotion just because you are aware of it, either. That's not for anyone else to decide. You get to make that choice. Only you. This trick buys you a few seconds to make that call. It gives you the chance to separate yourself from the emotion. Do you understand what that means?

You don't have to be the emotion anymore.

You can just be the person experiencing it, instead.

Get it?

I'm not asking you to bury your emotions here, pal. Quite the opposite, in fact. I'm asking you to fully acknowledge them. To feel them. And to know that *feeling* an emotion doesn't have to mean *becoming* the emotion. It doesn't have to mean reacting to it. It can simply mean asking the emotion what it is telling you, instead. All right?

Thank you for coming to my TED talk. More on this later.

I'll see you tomorrow.

Hi there, Trickster.

Come on in, buddy.

Guess what? I don't have anything for you to do today.

Really. Nothing.

I just want you to be here with me for a bit, pal. Stay here. Stay with me. Stay on this page. Just for now. Just for a few seconds. And breathe.

Slowly. Easily. There's no rush. Nothing to do. Nowhere to be.

Not for a few seconds, at least. For now, we just breathe.

Now look at that leaf. Look at it as it slowly falls to the ground.

Focus all of your attention on that leaf and picture it falling down from a big ol' oak tree.

Breathe in. Keep breathing in as it falls down. Slow down, buddy. Slow down. There.

It's on the ground.

You can breathe out now.

Slow and easy.

…And that's it.

That's all we were here to do today.

We were here to breathe. To give a few seconds of our day just to ourselves. Meant for nothing else. Meant for no one else. Except for being present with ourselves. And our bodies.

And tell you what, bud?

No matter what happens, remember this. Remember to keep breathing even when you feel like you can't. Especially when you feel like you can't. And I promise it will get better, okay? Immediately or slowly… It will get better. It always does. As long as you keep breathing.

Off you go now. Onto other things. Those emails aren't going to write themselves. I'll see you the day after.

HAPPINESS AND...
THE SELF

Hi there, Trickster.

Can you believe it? We are halfway done with our time together!

Sigh. I'm going to miss you when we're done, bud. Promise to visit me once in a while even then? Good. I can breathe a little better now.

I'd like to think that we are at a point right now where we can be honest about ourselves with each other. And I'd like to think that you feel that, too.

Today's task is going to require that of us, bud.

It's going to require us to be a little open. A little vulnerable.

Because today we are going to talk about our identities. Our identity is how we choose to authentically show up in the world every day. It is who we really are when we wake up every morning and before we go to sleep every night. It is who we are as a whole. Our personality, beliefs, quirks, vulnerabilities, desires, behaviours, choices, words, actions... All of it.

Identities are powerful.

And dynamic.

If we let them be.

Imagine, just for a moment, what it would be like if everyone could be who they would actually like to be all the time. If they could show up as themselves. Their true, authentic, weird, flawed, beautiful, evolving selves.

Without worry.

Without judgement.

Without apology.

Gosh. Can you sense the possibilities that would open up?

But because of this reality we live in, we sometimes put on masks to give cover to our true selves. We wear these masks to please others. To protect ourselves. To conform with norms. To make people comfortable. To avoid judgements. To fit in. To stand out.

These masks stop us from showing up in the world as our whole selves. They make us withhold parts of our being. They make us hide who we would really like to be. They make us create an illusion of who we think we should be. They are one of the biggest barriers we see on the road to happy living.

We all wear masks. Heck, we even have a closet full of them. We keep them carefully. Dust them ever so often. Make sure they keep looking good. Make sure they keep us looking good. Y'know what I mean?

Can I show you the mask I wear most often?

Beautiful, isn't it?

It took me years to make this.

Bit by bit. Corner by corner. Slowly. Carefully. Intentionally.

This is what I wear whenever I use humour to cover up my vulnerabilities. This is what I quickly put on every single time I crack a joke to keep others from seeing my true feelings. To keep a safe distance between myself and the world.

How many such masks are you wearing, pal?

Think about the times when you use anger to cover up sadness. Or when you use spite to hide your insecurities. And humour to keep people from getting too close to you. Think about the times that you pretend to be someone you're not. Or when you put yourself down to make room for others. And when you wear a mask of happiness all the time. Yep, you heard me. That's a mask too, bud. Of pretence. Of absolute perfection.

Think about all the sides of yourself that you hide from the world.

When you lock yourself in a small box of acceptable behaviours.

When you shrink yourself to comfort others.

When you stop yourself from truly being you.

You know what I'm talking about now. I know you do.

So, let me ask you again: How many masks are you wearing right now? How many do you have in storage? For emergencies? For certain people? For yourself? Would you like to make a list? I mean, it's always nice to have an inventory anyway, right?

SSH, HERE'S A SECRET INVENTORY OF ALL MY MASKS!

1. _____

2. _____

3. _____

4. _____

There you go.

I know Shakespeare said all the world's a stage, mate, but I think it may be time to stop acting now. Seriously. It's been five hundred years. I think it's safe for us to move on. Because these masks aren't helping anyone. Heck, they aren't even helping you.

Can I ask you to imagine something again?

Close your eyes. And imagine that you are at the dining table with everyone you care about. Even that one annoying cousin who secretly steals all of your chocolate from the fridge. Everyone's wearing their masks, aren't they? Because everyone's always wearing their masks. They keep adjusting their masks ever so often. Adding new feathers to them. Their hands are getting tired of holding them, but they don't let go. Can you see it?

Just then, the youngest kid at the table drops their mask on the floor.

Because it was really itching their skin. And limiting the amount of cake they could stuff in their mouths. And they just stand there. Cluelessly scratching their jaw. Eating their cake.

No one knows what to do. No one knows what to say. There's silence.

But a second later, someone else does it, too. They keep their mask down. Willingly. And so does the next person. And the next. And the next… Within a few seconds, everyone's real selves are out in the open. The strengths they have been afraid to use. The doubts they have been trying to hide. The potential they have left unexplored. The questions they would really like to ask. It's all out there. For everyone to see.

And, instead of judging each other, everyone just smiles and nods their heads in complete acceptance. In complete allowance. In complete celebration.

Sigh. How does that feel? Can you sense the joy?

Let me tell you something, mate: We weren't born with these masks. We were taught to put them on. We learned to put them on. We chose to put them on.

But do you know what that means?

We can take them off, too.

If we choose to.

If we allow ourselves to.

If we allow others to.

What do you say, bud?

Would you like to take off your mask and let the wind tickle your skin?

You don't have to decide right now.

Just think about it, ok?

I'll see you tomorrow.

Hi there, Trickster.

Crack those knuckles and take a seat, 'cause you are about to draw me a self-portrait with a twist. In just a moment.

You and I spoke a lot about masked identities yesterday, bub. We spoke about how they stop us from showing up as our authentic selves. From truly embracing who we really are. Then we closed our eyes and imagined a world where all of us would be able to take off our masks and share complete acceptance with each other. And celebrate each other.

What magic, right?

Which got me thinking…

If I were to take off my masks right now, who would I be? If I could truly be me, who would I choose to be? If you could truly be you, who would you choose to be?

Give it a thought, mate. In fact, let's think about it together. I mean, we've already shown all of our masks to each other. Might as well show our true selves too, right?

So, let's do this. Let's sketch ourselves our true identities.

Think about who you are. Think about who you would like to be. And all the values that you would like to embody. Think about all of those secret little things that are so important to you. And all of the big ones that the world already knows about. Think about what brings you joy. And what makes you angry. Think about how you want your eyes to shine. And for it to be a true reflection of what's on your mind. Think about all of this. And sketch me a portrait of your true self.

I'm not asking for a face here, pal. Do you realize that? I'm asking for you to show me what captures the essence of who you would like to show up as in the world. It could be a feather. An exclamation mark. Or three. Heck, it could be the entire cast of a Disney Pixar movie. Doesn't matter. As long as it captures you. With all of your quirks. Okay?

Let me ask you again: If you could truly be you, who would you choose to be? If you were to capture the essence of who you would like to show up as, what would that look like?

The page is yours, bud. Get at it.

Sigh. That's beautiful. I'm so proud of you.

I thought about it, too. Would you like to see what reflects the spirit of my true self?

There. Don't look at me with those big, confused eyes. I'll explain…

I sketched you a Baby Pegasus. Why? Hmm… Because a Pegasus is a winged stallion that speaks of freedom. It finds its gravity in flight. And flight, in gravity. A Pegasus is a self-aware and conscious being. It is kind, curious and creative. It walks the path of joy.

And that is how I would like to show up in the world, too. I would like to be free. And grounded. I would like to experience flight. And self-awareness. I would like to choose creativity and kindness whenever I can. Wherever I can. With whomever I can. I would like to look at the world with wonder. Take note of everything around me. And celebrate it. Fiercely.

My Pegasus identity is still a baby, though. Because my true self is that young, too. I still need to nourish it. Love it. Choose it. Play with it. Embrace it. And be kind to it.

This is my self-portrait with a twist, bub. Isn't it beautiful, too?

Go eat some chocolate oreo biscuits now, okay? You've earned it.

See you tomorrow.

Hi there, Trickster.

We have shared a couple of meaningful days this week, haven't we?

I celebrated after you left last night. I thought unmasking my true self called for it. So, I did something very significant. D'you know what?

I ate an entire cake!

Whaaa? Don't laugh at me!

I'm secretly your spirit animal and you know it. I know you do.

Anyway, I really thought the occasion called for it.

It was such a good cake. It had all of these different layers. A crunchy base. Fluffy chocolate pastry. Vanilla buttercream frosting. And some blueberries here and there, too. Yum. And look! I even saved you a piece. Aren't I the best? Are you sorry about laughing at me yet?

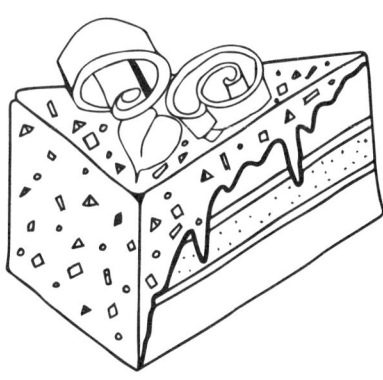

I was just sitting and eating this cake and thinking about all the different ingredients that made it so ridiculously delicious. Then, because my mind really likes to make associations, I started thinking about all the ingredients that make us who we are. You know what I mean?

Think of your ingredients as your roots, bud. They nourish your identity. Feed it food and water. Help it be. Grow. And change.

They could be anything. Everything. Our dreams. Values. Hopes. Flaws. Aspirations. Friends. Families. Our minds. Bodies. Experiences. Learnings. Setbacks. Our evolution.

Get what I mean?

So now, I have a very wacky question that I would like for you to answer: If you were a layer cake, which ingredients would make you who you really are?

Pick up your pencil and sketch it out for me, pal.

Sketch me a cake and talk to me about each layer.

Talk to me about the base that holds it together in place. That creates a foundation for you to exist and grow on. Maybe it's the people who support you. Who cheer for you. Or maybe it's just you, being the anchor you need yourself to be.

Talk to me about the pastry. What values have gone into giving it the flavour it has right now? Is it kindness that gives it such a sweet taste? And maybe, that slight tingly undertone is because honesty is there in the mix, too?

Then tell me about the frosting. Maybe your hopes give it that beautiful colour. And maybe your dreams are the sugary sparkly sprinkles on top of it.

And don't forget to sketch out those little treats that are hidden in the pastry and the frosting. Are those your life's experiences silently adding some flavour to the cake?

Go on, mate. Sharpen your pencil and get the sketch going. Draw a layer cake. And write little notes about each layer beside it. Take as much time as you need. Be as specific as you can. I mean, self-awareness is an important tool for a Trickster.

Wow. What a sight.

I'm going to sit here and stare at it for a while, okay?

Why don't you go eat the piece I set aside for you earlier?

Stuff your face. No one's looking.

I'll see you tomorrow.

Hi there, Trickster.

I have something special in store for you today.

Nope, it's not another piece of cake.

Come on. Do you really think I'm going to let myself get that predictable?

We have spent the last few days playing with our identities. We've dusted off our masks, caught glimpses of our true selves and acknowledged the sheer number of things that help make us who we really are. We've made inventories, self-portraits and uh... Cakes?

Wow. That sounds supremely weird.

How have you been putting up with me?

Anyway, I get that we have done a lot. And I get that there's still a whole lot that we can do. We can sit down with a pencil and talk some more. Make more lists. More drawings. Dig in deeper. But listen, what if we didn't? What if we didn't do any of that? What if we kept it as basic as we could? What say? You in? Yay! I'm glad.

Okay, so... What I want you to do today is to put in an official request.

Are you confused? Let me explain...

I want you to write an invitation letter, bud.

Write a letter to formally invite your authentic self to show up in the world. Invite all those parts of yourself that you have been hiding behind masks. That you have been rejecting. Because you don't see them fitting in. Because you don't see them being appreciated. Because they are flawed. And weird. And because... You know what? It doesn't matter. It really doesn't. Just invite all of them to show up. Invite all of you to show up.

Pick up the fanciest colours you can think of and get at it.

Make it heartfelt. And vibrant. Heck, maybe even stick a candy cane at the bottom. I mean, it has to be irresistible after all, right?

Let the record state that you are officially inviting yourself into the world.

Ready? How about I get the frame ready for you? I mean, it's the least I can do... There. All yours now...

Well, now how can anyone say no to that? You little charmer, you.

Remember to use this trick often, bub. Use it all the time. Whenever you feel like you are shrinking, okay? Once you regularly start inviting your true self to show up in the world, you don't need any of your masks anymore. You don't need any pretence. Because you are who you are. You are who you choose to be. Every minute. Every twenty-two and a half seconds.

And hey, I've been doodling an invitation letter of my own while you were busy writing. Look!

It's that letter from Hogwarts that never arrived.

Oh, psh! As if you never thought about which house you would be sorted into. Let me tell you something, of all the junk you can find on the Internet, those sorting hat quizzes are the only ones worth taking.

I even sketched myself a pet owl. Look how cute and fluffy it is!

Ugh. Fine. Laugh all you want.

Just get out of here and let me doodle in peace now, will you?

See you tomorrow.

Hi there, Trickster.

Come on in. Sit beside me.

I want to thank you today, mate. It's been quite a week for me. And I have really enjoyed it. Very much. It was the first time in a long while that I did not feel the absolute need to alternate between funny and serious. To make myself comfortable. And sometimes others, too. You know? So, thank you, bud. If no one's ever told you before: You are awesome.

Well, there's not much for us to do here right now. 'Cause I figured both of us could use some time off at this point. Ha. I'm pretty awesome myself, aren't I?

All I want you to do today is to turn it up. That's all. Just turn up the volume of who you really are. Go all the way. As far as you can.

Let's do this, yeah? Let's do it together.

Lie down. Or stand up. Or keep sitting. Doesn't matter. Just be at ease. And close your eyes. Take a moment to get comfortable with yourself. With the quiet. And the stillness. Be present with it. Be present with you. Take as long as you would like to.

And then step past all of the masks that you have on right now. Step beyond all the judgements. Fears. Expectations. All the different points of view. The drama. Step past all of it. Picture yourself walking away from it. Step by step. Treading lightly. At your own pace.

Keep walking till you reach the space where your true self lives. This is the place inside of you that you feel most at home with. This is where you feel free. Fierce. Limitless. And true.

There are no masks here.

There's no one else here, either.

It's just you. And all the different parts of you. Those that you have embraced. Those that you have celebrated. And those that you haven't even acknowledged yet. Those that you may have even denied. They are all here. Together. For you.

Can you see it?

Now, turn to your right. Imagine a big silver dial there. Which controls the extent to which your true self shows up in the world. Walk over to it. Notice where it's set at right now.

Touch the dial. See how it feels. Is it cold? Warm?

Wrap your fingers around it. Then slowly, turn it up. Keep turning it as far up as it goes. Keep going... And just when you feel like you must stop, turn it over a little bit more. Just a little... And you're done.

That's it.

Tell me where you left it? Mark it here.

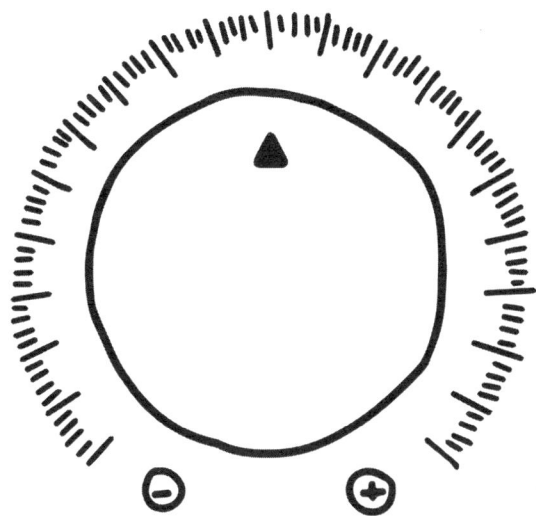

Heh! That makes me happy.

This is all I wanted us to do today, bud.

Remember to visit this place often.

And every time you are here, turn it up. And show up. Okay?

I'm going to take a nap now.

See you tomorrow.

Hi there, Trickster.

Grab a chair and let's talk, yeah?

Before you came in, I had all kinds of crazy ideas in mind for today. But it can all wait for now. Because I think this is a very good time for us to pause for a moment and take stock of where we are at. And how we are feeling about everything that we have done.

I mean, we are a little beyond the halfway point of our journey together, bud. Did you realize that?

We are at a point where we have actually begun to do stuff. We have begun to get out of our own way. We have begun to create things. Possibilities. Joy. Gratitude. Magic. And more space for ourselves and our choices.

And I can't help but wonder: How are you feeling about everything? Are there any shifts in your world at all? In your mind? Are you having any doubts? Is your inner critic quiet? Or is it sending all kinds of nasty thoughts your way? Has perfectionism knocked on your door? Have you been able to keep up with some of your daily practices?

Maybe it's a good time for us to do a quick check-in. Sometimes it just helps to know.

Don't overthink this exercise. Just follow your gut and show me what you are feeling about everything, using my old and trusted yay-meh-nay scale.

Circle yay for good. Meh for neutral. And nay for bad.

Got it? Start rating!

Yay   Meh   Nay
making room for courage

Yay   Meh   Nay
thinking of judgements as points of view

Yay   Meh   Nay
keeping my inner critic quiet

Yay   Meh   Nay
prioritising mental health

Yay   Meh   Nay
asking for emotional support

Yay   Meh   Nay
using my gratitude rock

Yay   Meh   Nay
turning conclusions into questions

Yay   Meh   Nay
keeping my barrier wall down

Yay   Meh   Nay
naming emotions

Yay   Meh   Nay
staying curious

Yay   Meh   Nay
being kind to myself

Yay   Meh   Nay
being generally awesome

I hear you, pal. I do.

Thanks for being honest.

You're the best.

And hey, listen?

Keep checking in every now and then to see if you are making any progress, all right? Enjoy your day off tomorrow.

See you the day after.

HAPPINESS AND...
CONFIDENCE

Date: / /   **Week 7: Confidence**

Hi there, Trickster.

Welcome back! Come sit next to me.

Careful! Watch your step.

Walk in nice and slow. I don't want you to trip and fall on your nose. I like your nose. It's cute. So, let's not break it today, okay?

What? Stop looking at me with those confused eyes.

I make sense. Promise.

Look! Do you see that ladder in the middle of the room? I just want you to be careful around it. That's all. I'm a nice and concerned talking book, aren't I?

Isn't it pretty? I have an inkling it's upside down. But still. So pretty.

Do you know what it's called?

The Ladder of Self-Confidence.

Ah! That has such a nice little ring to it, doesn't it?

And guess what? I ordered it especially for you!

Don't you just adore me?

Say yes. Say it. SAY IT.

Good. Ahem. Let's quickly move past that, yeah?

So, the ladder. I have heard great things about it. As it turns out, it can be a very good tool for self-reflection. And after we are done reflecting, we can always climb on it and pretend to be Simba from *The Lion King*. What fun, right?

Now, I want you to look at this Ladder of Self-Confidence and tell me where you are standing on it right now. Just look at each step. See what it means for you. Trust your gut; there's no science behind it, no fancy formulas that I can offer just yet. You will just have to tell me what you know.

What I know is that the topmost rung of the ladder represents a wholesome communion between you and your true self. That's the step you arrive at when you experience absolute ease with being yourself. Even in situations that aren't easy. You arrive there when you embrace the strength of your voice. When judgements stop yielding much power over you. When all of your barriers are down. When you honour who you are. And when you take up space. When you continue to show up. And when you have complete awareness of all the choices that are available to you.

That's where we would like to get to, of course.

But to do that, we have to ask ourselves: Where are we right now?

So, do that. Ask yourself some questions. Ask: 'Where am I right now? What would it take for me to reach the next step? Are there any barriers that are stopping me from getting there? What are they? What can I do to get past them? Are there any tools available to me that can help me with that?'

Maybe you have a feeling that you are two levels away from the topmost rung. And maybe you know that it's because you still get bogged down by judgements. There's nothing wrong with that. You just need to practise. Maybe you can try lowering your barriers. Or you can practise looking at judgements as points of view. Or you can use some affirmations. Try a mix of different things. And be curious to find out what will work the best. Okay?

Come on, now. Answer me this: Where are you standing on the ladder right now?

_____

_____

_____

_____

Okay. Cool.

Now tell me this: What is stopping you from going just one step higher? Do you know which barriers stand in your way? Take a moment and consider this. Close your eyes and think about all those moments when you have felt yourself shrink because you haven't been able to be yourself. When you have felt the joy just being sucked out of your life. What stopped you? Was it fear? Some labels? Lack of emotional support? Or something else? Write it all down.

WHAT'S STOPPING ME FROM GOING HIGHER ON
THE LADDER OF SELF-CONFIDENCE?

1. _____

2. _____

3. _____

4. _____

I hear you, bud. Here's my final question: Are there any tools currently available to you that you can use to get rid of these barriers? Maybe some that we have spoken of in the last six weeks. Or some that you have gathered from your mentors, friends and family. Maybe even off the Internet. Or a few that you just intuitively know will work for you. Make a note of them.

WOULD YOU LOOK AT MY COOL TOYS? I MEAN TOOLS!

1. _____

2. _____

3. _____

4. _____

All right. I see what you mean.

And there you have it. So much information. Where you're at. What's stopping you. And all the tools that you know will work for you. Play with them often. And tell me how it turns out. Tell me if it brings more joy into your life.

And if you need some help thinking of a few more tools, ask for it. Go talk to someone. Hit people up. Reach out to your tribe. Your favourite human. Your parents. Or best friend. A professional. Maybe your mentors. Or your siblings. Just go talk to someone, okay?

That's all for today, bud. We are done reflecting now. We know. And now that that's out of the way, I'm going to go watch *The Lion King*. Maybe in Spanish?

See you tomorrow.

Hi there, Trickster.

I have been thinking a lot since I woke up this morning. About this strange, strange journey that we are on. And the stranger thing we call belief. Belief in others. In situations. And in ourselves.

Well, mostly in ourselves.

Before we began this ride, the biggest thing that stopped me from truly being happy was the lack of belief I had cultivated for myself. I would walk around with this weird idea of being wrong. Do you get what I mean? It was a very interesting point of view for me to have.

I was wrong for being who I was. I was wrong for believing in what I believed in. I was wrong for making the choices I made. I was wrong for trying the things I tried. I was wrong for doing the things I did. I was wrong for using my voice. I was wrong for showing up. I was wrong for not showing up. I was wrong for taking up space. I was wrong for being too much. I was wrong for being too less. I was wrong. Always wrong. Always wrong.

Sigh. That word held so much significance in my life.

I think it took me the last seven weeks to finally realize that sometimes it's harder for us to acknowledge all that is right about us. All that is good about us. All that is great about us. Sometimes, it might be easier for us to just accept that we are wrong. Without ever questioning it. You know?

Don't get me wrong, though. I'm not talking about making mistakes here. That's completely different. We all make mistakes. Of course we do. We all slip up from time to time. In work. In relationships. And I understand the importance of owning up to it and offering a meaningful apology in those situations. But that's a whole different conversation. That's not what we are dealing with right now. What I'm talking about is an inherent belief of being wrong. A belief that tells you that who you truly are is wrong. Get it?

It was one of the biggest 'I am...' labels of my life. One of the biggest lies I told myself. And one of the biggest self-limiting thoughts I bought into.

Now I don't know what it looks like for you bud, but do something with me? Write 'I am not wrong' as many times as you can. And know that the 'I' you are talking about is your true and authentic self. That 'I' may be flawed. It may make mistakes. It may slip up. But it is not wrong. Do you hear me? It is not wrong. You are not wrong.

Write it down. And know that when you say it, all you mean is that you are not wrong for being who you are. Write it till you believe it. Write it till it seeps into your consciousness. Write it till it becomes true for you. Fill every page of this book with it if you need to. Scribble it in every corner. Use up the margins. Shout. Whisper. Do what you must. Do it now.

Start writing with me and then take over on your own.

I am not wrong. I am not wrong. I am not wrong. I am not wrong.

I am not…

Sigh. Say it once more. With me. Please?

I may be flawed. I may make mistakes. But I am not wrong.

I am not wrong.

Damn. That feels good, doesn't it?

Go drink some tea to celebrate this moment.

Whoops! I almost spilled it. My mistake. I'm sorry. Drink it up!

I'll see you tomorrow.

Hi there, Trickster.

Clap your hands and close your eyes because I have a surprise for you!

Or on second thought, don't.

Otherwise, I might just sketch long whiskers on your face with a permanent red marker. Don't ask me why. Do you think I have reasons to do this kind of stuff? Of course not. It's just something I must do.

Stop shaking your head at me and focus on the surprise. Look!

It's a cupcake! Yum! And it's fresh out of the oven, too. Well, at least that's what it said at the bakery.

Don't you just love surprises? I know I do. They lift my spirits. And make me grin. Sometimes clap. And I always end up feeling a whole lot better about everything else that's happening in my life. And that's exactly what we are here to do today.

We are here to create some surprises for ourselves.

Excited? Me too!

So, here's the deal: In a perfect world, all of us would be standing at the highest step on the Ladder of Self-Confidence.

Well, at least we are on our way there, right?

But you know what? Even when we get there, wouldn't it be kind of nice to be surprised by some simple pick-me-ups every now and then? What do you say we make some today? Yeah?

We are going to write ourselves some encouraging notes. Nothing too big. Nothing fancy. Just little notes of happiness. And then we are going to cut them out and hide them. Where? In our socks. Under our pillows. In our pockets. Between our clothes. Somewhere in our books. In boxes of sweets. I don't know. Go wild with ideas here.

And then a few days or weeks from now, when we find these notes, we are going to do a quick dance and hide them someplace new again. We are going to let those notes keep surprising us. Keep bringing us little nuggets of joy. And be our own little pick-me-ups. All right?

Don't think too much about what to write.

Let it be silly. Let it be weird. Let it be anything.

All it has to do is bring a smile on your face. That's all.

Here, let me get you started with some.

May a puppy wag its tail at you today.

You go, human!

Jump on some leaves today!

Got some ideas? Now you go! Write some more.

Now, get some paper and write ten more. And leave them for strangers to find in different places. Like coffee houses. Or book shops. Cafes. Markets. Buses. Taxis. Anywhere.

Ssh! Do it. Just don't litter, okay?

Out you go.

See you tomorrow.

Hi there, Trickster.

Something very strange happened after you left last night.

I was hiding my notes of happiness in all kinds of different places. Like in the fridge. And under the mattress. In pillowcases. And behind paintings. You know, the usual. When all of a sudden, I was hit by a question: When was the last time I truly believed in myself?

When was the last time I stood at the topmost step on the Ladder of Self-Confidence? When was the last time I could be myself without any apology? Any excuses? When was the last time I felt that kind of joy?

I think it was when I was still a child. Maybe when I was about seven. And I realized that all I have been trying to do since then is to recall that sense of absolute ease with which I could be myself. I have been trying to remember what that felt like. And I have been trying to relive it.

Which made me wonder…

If I were to ever meet that seven-year-old version of me, what would that experience be like? What would it say to me? Would it ask me to do something differently? Would it ask me to do something I haven't done in years? Would it have any questions for me? Would I have any questions for it? And what would it say about this journey of happy living that we are on?

Do you have a sense of what I'm talking about? And are you curious enough to find out?

Yes? Good.

So, let's do something now, okay?

Let's have a conversation with the seven-year-old versions of ourselves. Right now.

Are you ready?

Close your eyes. Breathe deep. And remember the kind of faith you had in yourself when you were a child. When you thought that anything was possible. When there was wonder all around you. When you thought you could be a superhero if you wanted to. Heck, you could be anything you wanted to. When you had no judgements about yourself. When you could laugh the loudest in a room and not give a damn about what anyone else would think. When you didn't care about embarrassing yourself. Especially if it meant having some fun. When you didn't feel the need to pay any attention to your inner critic. And when the idea of perfectionism didn't exist in your life. When you believed in yourself. Without cause. When you were gentle with yourself. And when showing up simply meant walking inside a room. When you could be yourself. Your weird, flawed, wonderful, evolving self. Without apology. Without reason. Without excuses. Remember that?

Now imagine meeting that version of you. Notice the sparkle in their eyes. Say hello. Sense the curiosity with which they are looking at you. The softness. And imagine what they would say to you. Write it down. Like a letter.

From them to you. From you to you. Write a letter of encouragement. And wonder. Of acceptance. And allowance.

Pick up your pencil. Listen closely. And write...

Oh, wow. Now that's a voice I would listen to all day long.
  Why don't you go back and read it once more?
  Maybe sit on some swings while you do that?

Or maybe not.
  Looks like it's occupied.
  Just sit on the floor, okay?
  I'll see you tomorrow.

Hi there, Trickster.

Wasn't it a different kind of incredible to meet our weird, flawed and wonderful younger selves yesterday? And let's admit it: There's so much that we can learn from these versions of ourselves, right? About authenticity. About using our voices. And about showing up. Do you get what I mean?

I have been thinking about that last bit for quite some time now, bud. I have been talking about it over hot cocoa with friends. Writing emails to kind humans who can help me understand it just a little bit better. And I think I finally have a pretty good idea of what it means now. I could use some new words to explain it to you, but will you let me do something else instead? Will you let me read to you from a book that I have become recently acquainted with? Good.

The book is called *Big Magic*. We spoke about it before, remember? And Elizabeth Gilbert is the wonderful, wonderful human who brought it into the world. She talks about something called creative entitlement, which I think perfectly captures the essence of showing up in the world. She says that it doesn't mean 'acting as though the world owes you anything whatsoever. No, creative entitlement simply means believing that *you are allowed to be here*, and that—merely by being here—you are allowed to have a voice and a vision of your own.'

Wow, amirite?

When I read those lines for the first time, it blew my mind. Straight out of the window. It moved oceans in my heart. And created more room for freedom in my world. For me in my world. Know what I mean? And does that sound like a thing you would like to experience too?

Do something with me then. Show up. And declare that you are here. That you are allowed to be here. With your voice. With your vision. With your questions.

Close your eyes, bud. I don't have any markers on me, so you're safe. Keep them closed. And breathe. You know the drill by now. Breathe. And let a sense of calm surround you completely. Let it fill you. Slowly. Slowly. Now, go back to the place where your true self lives.

You know the way. You were there only last week.

Find your way back to that place again.

Take your time.

…Are you there? Good.

This is you. Your true 'I'. This is where you live.

Now imagine that this true self of yours is getting bigger and bigger. Taking more and more space. Stretching out in all directions.

Let it grow. More. More. More.

And just when you think that it must stop, give it permission to grow just a little bit more. Let it move around. And get comfortable with all the space it has now.

And now open your eyes. And repeat after me.

I am here. I am here. I am right here.

Write it and scribble it on every corner of this page. Fill every blank space with these words. Start with me and then continue on your own.

I am here. I am here. I am

You are here.

Hi. I see you. You are here.

Do this every day. Say this every day. Tell yourself that you are here. And that you are allowed to have a voice and a vision of your own. Declare it. Okay?

Would you like to shout it out from the windows now?

Go. I'll throw 'em open for you.

Ha! Now wasn't that just positively dramatic?

Get out of here, bud.

I'll see you tomorrow.

Hi there, Trickster.

Here it is again: The end of another (hopefully) amazing week.

We have spent the last five days believing in ourselves. We have stepped on ladders. And pretended to be Simba. We have shown up. Flexed our muscles. And taken up space. We have used our voices. Met our younger selves. And shared top secret conversations. We have written letters. And small notes of encouragement. Eaten cupcakes. Made some meaningful declarations.

You know, same old, same old.

All of this has left me wondering: If you were to flip your way back to the beginning of our journey and read the permission slip you wrote for yourself at the end of the first week, would there be anything that you'd like to change? Anything at all?

I mean, we have been at this for almost two months now, bub. And after all that you know yourself to be at this point, isn't there anything else that you would like to give yourself the permission to do? And be?

Maybe you would like to tell yourself that it's okay to be seen. And that it's okay to use your voice. To be different. To be you. All of you. Without any apology. Or maybe you would just like to remind yourself of a few things that you have forgotten over the course of the last seven weeks.

Why don't you go on and do that now?

Why don't you write yourself a brand new permission slip?

Give yourself more freedom than you did in the first week. Do you hear me? Allow yourself to be more of who you truly are. Create more room for your choices. Your emotions. Remember to acknowledge every emotion. Even the unpleasant ones. And remind yourself to take off your masks. To turn it up. To breathe. Tell yourself that you are not wrong. And then have allowance for yourself when you make mistakes. Be gentle. And kind. With yourself. With others. Remind yourself to cultivate a sense of creative entitlement. And let the world know that you are here. Heck, maybe even let yourself know you are here.

I'll leave it to you, bud. I mean, it's not like I want to tell you what to write…

Did I just say that out loud? With a straight face?

HA. I'm the worst, aren't I?
You ready?
Here we go...

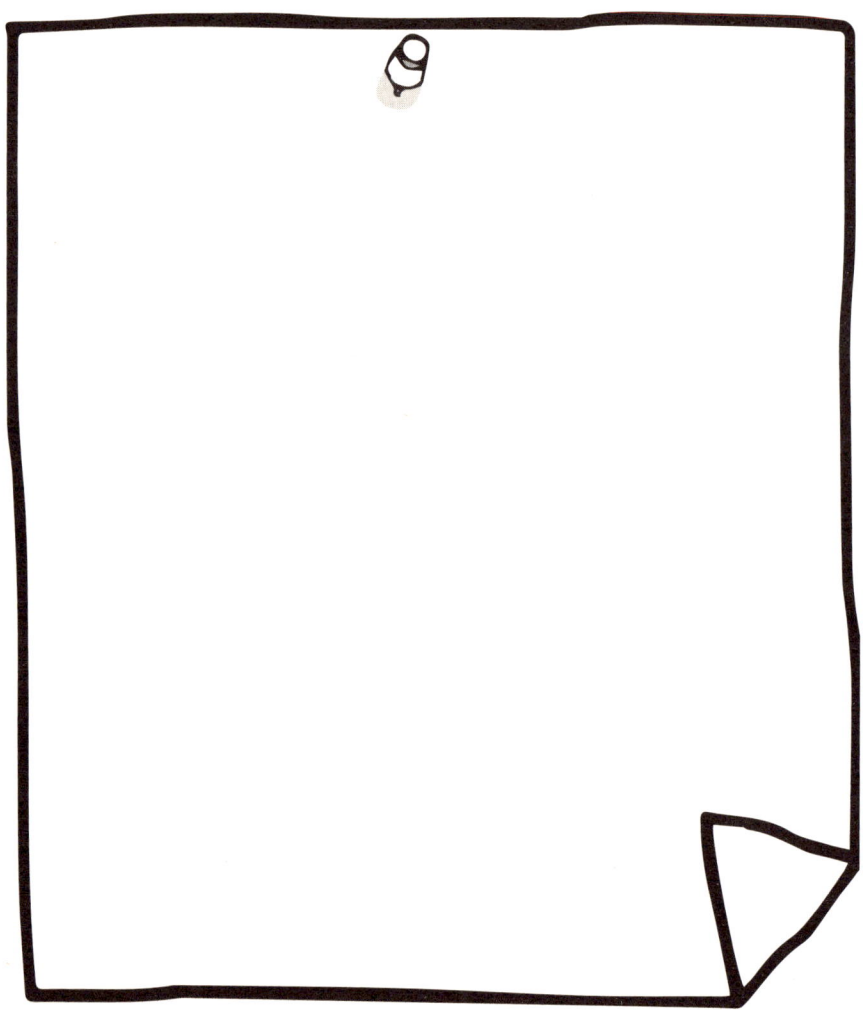

Sigh. Just look at that.
What a beauty. Why don't you laminate it? Maybe even get it insured?
I'm going to redo mine now, okay?
See you the day after.

HAPPINESS AND...
CREATIVITY

Hi there, Trickster.

Can you believe we are going to spend six whole days talking about creativity?
Ha! Me neither. Gosh, it's going to be amazing, isn't it?
Huh? What's that? What's creativity got to do with happy living, you ask?
Well, as it turns out, a whole freakin' lot.
It lifts your spirits. Calms your mind. Makes you a lot more curious. Keeps you present in the moment. And makes you notice all of the small things around you. Know what I'm saying? It nudges you to get more comfortable with uncertainty. And unfamiliarity. It makes you surrender. And get out of your own damn way. So that you can begin to see new solutions to old problems. New possibilities to say yes to. New questions to ask. And new adventures to go on. And isn't that exactly what we have been trying to do here since the first day?
Heck, you could even call this entire journey an exercise in creative living.
Because creativity is a muscle. That you have been using to look at things in a different way. That you have been moving to gather more tricks for your toolbox. That you have been flexing since the moment we started talking.
So, it doesn't really matter if you can tap dance to a Broadway Musical or not.
If you can write a sonnet like Shakespeare or not.
Or if you can paint like Frida Kahlo or not.
You can still be creative.
You can still use the tools of art to build that muscle.
You don't have to be good at it. You just have to be willing to give it a go.
Isn't that neat?
So what say, bud? Are you ready to begin this week on creativity?
Woohoo! Me, too!

Hm, where do we start?

Oh, I know! Tell me: Do you hear that? No?

THAT! How are you missing that sound?

Wow! We need to work on this. Right away.

Close your eyes for a minute. Be still. And listen to all of the sounds around you. Listen to the sound of the floor creaking. Or of the car honking outside your building. Listen to the soft crackle of electricity. And to the almost absent sound of the air inside the room. And hey, pay close attention: Is that someone playing with their keys in the distance? Be silent. And focus. Listen to as many different sounds as you can. Register them. And then note them down here.

WHOA, THESE ARE THE SOUNDS I CAN ACTUALLY HEAR!

1. _____

2. _____

3. _____

4. _____

Oh, more?

5. _____

6. _____

7. _____

Now pick the fourth sound on your list and write a five-line mystery thriller around it. I don't know how. Just make it happen.

Remember: Your job is to write the story; not to judge it. Go!

There you go.

I'll say it again: You really are smarter than I first thought you were.

IT'S A COMPLIMENT.

Heh. Go learn how to say thank you.

I'll see you tomorrow.

Hi there, Trickster.

Do you like making new friends?

    Because that's what we are here to do today.

    I want you to sketch me a monster.

    Yep, you heard me.

    Sketch me a monster. But, like, don't give it very sharp teeth. Or spikes instead of hair. Or an axe to carry around. You get what I mean, don't you? Just make sure it's friendly.

    Go on. Pick up your pencil. Get at it.

Oh, hi! Welcome to the world!

    What's our new friend called? _____.

    What a cool name.

    I think we should start getting to know our buddy a little better, don't you?

    So, this is what's going to happen now: I'm going to give you a bunch of questions to ask the monster, okay? Just read them out for our friend. Listen closely for the answers. And note them down. That's all.

    Remember: These questions are not for you to answer. They are for the monster. All you are doing is writing down the responses. Nothing else. Capeesh?

Yes, I know it sounds silly, bud. But play along. For me?

Look at the drawing you made. Invite it for a conversation. Offer it some tea. Ask the questions. And jot down the first thing you hear in your mind. Begin!

1. How old are you? _____

2. Do you have a favourite flavour of ice cream? _____

3. What do you like the most about your favourite movie? _____

4. Do you have any siblings? Tell me something about them. _____
   _____

5. Who are you closest to in your family? What's your fondest memory of
   them? _____

6. Tell me something about your best friend. What do you like the most about
   them? And the least? _____
   _____

7. When was the last time that you lied? Why? Did you get away with it?
   _____

8. What are you most scared of? _____

9. Did you ever have braces as a child? _____

10. Do you have a secret that you can share with me?_____
    _____

11. When was the last time you cried? Why? _____
    _____

12. What makes you angry? _____
    _____

13. Is there a meal that reminds you of your childhood? Who used to cook it
    for you? _____

14. If you were to see a pebble on the road, would you kick it or walk past it?

Ha! There you go. I think we have asked enough questions for now.

Tell me, bud: Do you realize what just happened here?

A simple drawing became a distinct character. With some depth. With a past. And a set of likes and dislikes. Some quirks. And a unique personality.

How do you think that happened? What did we do to make it happen?

You know it. We became curious. We asked questions. Lots of them. And with each question, we learned a little bit more. We created more fodder to feed our creativity. We made more room to play with the character. We noticed the smaller details. And we became truly present with the moment. Isn't that nice?

Are there any more questions that you want to ask? Why don't you go do that now?

Just feed the monster some sugar first.

I'll see you tomorrow.

Hi there, Trickster.

Are you prepared for today to be absolutely bonkers?

No, seriously. Are you?

Well, you should be.

Because we are going to play my favourite improve game. Isn't that exciting?

Gosh! Can't. Stop. Grinning.

I have so many fond memories of this game, bud. I used to play it with my friends all the time when I was younger. We would play this whenever we were feeling a little stuck. Or like we were out of new ideas. Or like we wanted to control everything around us. And do you know what the best part was? It didn't require us to do any preparation. We would just gather around in a circle and get at it. I think it helped us get more comfortable with the big, scary idea of the uncertain. And it made us celebrate the unfamiliar. And look at failure differently, too.

…Is that a lot of words? I feel like that was a lot of words.

You know what? Forget everything I just said. And start to think of it as a fun exercise. That's all. A fun little exercise that can introduce an explosion of new possibilities to any moment, conversation or situation that you are in.

There. That's a lot better. I was worried about overselling it to you for a bit. Thank goodness, I reeled it in.

Anyhoo, does that sound like something you would like to experience?

Here's how this is going to work: You and I are going to build a story together. You are going to be the chief narrator. Sounds fancy, dunnit? And I am going to be the navigator with this ultra-cool compass. Look!

Ready? No? Let me explain…

I'm going to sit back and listen while you create a story. Any story. And then every now and then, whenever I feel like it, I'm going to step in and offer a question. Or a suggestion. This will be something that can change the entire direction of the story.

And like I said, I can do this whenever I want. Even if you are in the middle of a sentence. Or a really cool plot point. Okay? And every single time I do this, you simply have to say 'yes, and…' to continue the story from where I left off. Get it?

You narrate.

I navigate.

And you narrate, again.

So, say, you start with something like this: 'It was a beautiful sunny morning and Gee was excited about going to the airport.' And then, I suddenly step in and say: 'Ooh! And then the bear knocked on her door and asked her for some breakfast.' You just have to take that prompt and let it change the direction of your story. You could say: 'Yes, exactly! And then after she calmed down and stopped screaming, she served the bear some pancakes with honey.'

Or something along those lines.

There's really no way for you to get this wrong, bud. You can be as wacky as you like. Or serious. Sweet. Funny. Intelligent, even. It's completely up to you. Except when it's up to me. But after that, it's completely up to you again. All right?

Let me start by pointing us in a general direction. And then you can step in and take over.

Ahem, ahem. Here goes: Gee woke up one morning with a huge grin on her face. 'This is it,' she said. 'Today is the day I'm finally going to…'

COME ON. What next? Over to you now, mate.

And just then, a big strawberry fell on her head. Out of nowhere. And then ten more…

Gosh! How did so much happen already? Anyway, tell me: isn't that exactly when she decided to go and buy some Harry Potter memorabilia for herself?

Yes! And that's when the door opened and S walked in with a monkey, isn't it?

Well, if you think about it, Gee knew exactly what she had to do. Why else would she pick up the phone and punch in that familiar number?

'No way! My wand can't be real,' she screamed. But as soon as she said that, she saw a tiny yellow spark... Oh, no...

Wait, wait, wait. All of that's great, but what the heck was a purple talking giraffe doing in the middle of her living room? How did it even fit in?

'Ha!' thought the giraffe, as it poked its head out of the window and spotted the hot air balloon. 'Not so fast,' it muttered.

My head is spinning. But I must ask: Is this when Gee held her stomach and laughed so hard that the water she was drinking started to come out of her nose?

Okay, I need to know: What happened to S? And where did all of those birds come from?

I see. And was that when Gee finally decided to buy some land on the moon?

The end. HAHAHAHAHAHAHA.

Wasn't that fun? Didn't you want to smack me across the head when I introduced the talking purple giraffe? I knew it. I could see it in your eyes.

But don't you see? This is what makes this game work! It makes you use all of those crazy first ideas that you would otherwise ignore. It nudges you to get out of your head. And trust your instincts. It allows you to step out of form. And structure. Into the unknown. Out of your own way. And d'you know what else it does? It makes you curious about new possibilities. It makes you keep your eyes open. So that you can say: 'Huh. What if I took this further? What if I just trusted my gut and said yes? I wonder...' Get it?

It makes you remember to say yes to new ideas when you would like to. And to not let fear or hesitation stop you.

That's all for today, bud.

I'm going to polish my compass now. It's getting a little rusty.

Why don't you read our masterpiece again?

Maybe even cut it out and put it up on the fridge?

See you tomorrow.

Hi there, Trickster.

Stop whatever you are doing right now.

I mean it. Stop. Good.

Now pick up a pencil. Or some paints and brushes. Maybe even some crayons. And get out of here. Literally. Get out of this room. And step out into the open. Go to a park, a balcony, or a roof.

Come on. Out you go. I'm waiting…

Are you there yet? Cool.

Now look up. Can you see the sky? Move a little if you need to. Just make sure you have a clear view of it. Done?

What does it look like?

No, no. Don't tell me. Show me. Sketch it for me. Or paint it. Or write about it. It doesn't matter what you do. As long as you show me what you see. Begin!

Sigh. Isn't that a beauty?

I'm so proud of you, fam.

You know what? There are probably tens of millions of people who have sketched, painted or written about the sky before you did today. And there will probably be another tens of millions of people who are going to do it again in the future.

But no one has ever done it like you before.

And no one ever will.

Which is what makes this piece yours. And only yours.

I know of so many people who absolutely refuse to be creative because they think they can never be original and create something new. And guess what? Most of the time, they are right. In all likelihood, they can't be original. But why on earth should that mean that they can't be creative, either?

Think about it. Every book has already been written. Every movie has already been made. Every song has already been sung. I mean, we are more than several thousand years into the future and we are still talking about the same things our ancestors did.

And why shouldn't we? Maybe there's nothing 'new' left for us to talk about. Nothing 'original' we can think of. You know, whatever that word means.

Who cares if you want to tell a story that has already been told?

Tell it again. And tell it your way.

Use your voice. Your vision. Your expression. Your heart.

I'm not asking you to become lazy and stop thinking for yourself. You realize that, right? And I'm not asking you to become a thief and steal other people's work, either. Far from it. All I'm saying is this: Create what you would like to create in the way that only you would create it. That's all.

Ask the same questions, if you must. Explore the same motives. Talk about the same feelings. Tell the same stories. But make it yours. Put your voice in it. Put your heart in it. Put yourself in it. Okay? Trust me. That's all that matters.

Now get out of here and enjoy the view.

I'll see you tomorrow.

Hi there, Trickster.

Do you want to know what's on my mind today?

Yes, you're right: Facebook asked me that question.

And no, I'm not thinking about food. Well, not yet, at least.

Can I start talking now?

Something about this week is making me think a lot about my own creative process. You see, when I was younger, I attached a lot of anxiety to the process of beginning a new project. Or even continuing an old one. I don't quite know how to explain it, bud. Everything about it just seemed so daunting.

And why wouldn't it? Isn't starting a new project much like walking up to a random person on the street and tapping them on their shoulder to say: 'Hi, there. You seem interesting. Let's chat for the next few months.'

Gah! Awkward much? What if they say no? What if they don't want to talk? Dang it, what if they call the cops?

It wasn't very easy for me to start having a creative conversation with an idea. To start asking it questions like we did earlier this week. There was too much of a burden attached to it. Too many expectations. Too many judgements.

And well, it certainly did not help when I let perfectionism take a vote. Or when I handed my inner critic a microphone to talk through.

So I just ignored new ideas. And pushed back old projects. And that was that for a few years. Things started to change when a friend of mine started to question all the conclusions and assumptions I was making. They sat me down and asked: 'What has creation become for you? How can you begin enjoying it again? Is there something beyond all the conclusions, judgements, fears and assumptions you are hiding behind?'

Damn it. What if there really was something beyond all of it?

So, I stood up. Dusted my pants. Put a toe forward. And started looking around.

And slowly, I realized that the burden of starting a creative conversation had never been on me in the first place. No one expected that of me. It wasn't in my job description when I signed up to live creatively. I was only assuming and concluding that it was.

Do you know what was actually asked of me?

To show up and join a conversation that was already happening around me. To say 'yes, and…' to take it forward if I could. That's all.

That didn't seem as scary. In fact, it didn't seem scary at all.

You see fam, we don't exist in isolation. And our ideas don't, either. There are triggers all around us. We are living in a world where creative conversations are happening all the time. They are happening everywhere. And whenever an idea strikes us, we have already become a part of that conversation. From there, it's up to us to choose. To say yes or no. To contribute to it or bow out from it. It really is that simple.

Think about it, bub. You have created a whole lot for yourself in the last eight weeks. How?

By taking every single prompt that was offered to you and saying yes to it. By choosing to continue a conversation that you did not begin. And if all that creation means is contributing to an ongoing conversation, then maybe it doesn't have to be a lonely walk through a minefield. Maybe it can be a fun adventure through a corn maze, instead. The question is: Will you let it be that?

That's all I want to say to you today, bud. I want you to remember this. I want you to feel like you have the license to enter any creative conversation that is happening on this planet. And to raise your hand politely and say something to contribute to it. Stand silently and learn from it. Or to bow your head and depart from it, okay?

And because I'm kinda awesome, I went ahead and got it officially printed for you. Look!

It's a real creative license! Aren't I simply adorable?

Now go get a tiny photograph of yours. Stick it on. Enter all of your details. And then cut the license out and keep it with you. Forever. Keep it in a place you visit often. So that you can see it regularly. And let it remind you that creativity is simply saying yes or no to the offer of continuing a conversation you did not begin. The rest will take care of itself. It always does.

Go on now. Fill it up. Cut it out. Maybe even laminate it?

I'll leave you to it.

See you tomorrow.

Hi there, Trickster.

I can't believe it's the end of the week already. Where did all that time fly off to, amirite? I don't want to start crying. So, let's just move on to what we are here to do today, okay?

Have you ever thought of having a creator's signature?

Wait a minute. Do you even know what that is?

A creator's signature is a way for you to leave behind your mark on a piece of work. It's a way for you to communicate what creation means to you. Think of it like this: If your creative work were a living, breathing life form, then this signature would be the secret language you would use to speak about your partnership. It would mean something.

Now I'm not talking about scribbling your name on the bottom of every page that you write. Although if that's what you are inclined to do, then by all means, go for it. Go for anything. Think of a stroke, symbol, smudge, design, word or anything else that communicates the relationship you share with creativity.

I know of a brilliant artist who signs her paintings with her thumbprints. She camouflages it so beautifully in the bottom right corner of all of her canvases that most people don't even realize something's there.

But you see, that's the whole point. It doesn't matter to her if others can see it or not. She doesn't do it for them. She does it for herself. And her creation. She does it to leave behind a small mark which reminds her that she had said yes to this idea before. That she had been here before. And that being here had meant something to her. Creation had meant something to her. Big or small, spectacular or ordinary, doesn't matter... It had meant something.

Would you like to have something similar in your life, too? Would you like to play with different ideas right now? And discover what your creator's signature looks like?

Get your toolbox, then. You know, your pencils, paints, crayons... And just start trying out all kinds of things. Know that there's no wrong way to go about it. Try a bunch of different things and trust that you will know when you arrive at your signature. Okay? You will just know.

And hey, remember that you can change it anytime you want. I mean, if the way we feel about creation changes ever so often, why shouldn't the signature?

Go on now. Roll up your sleeves. And be prepared to get your hands dirty. Take to the page. And make it yours. Go!

Whoa. That's one vibrant page, isn't it?

Tell me, bud: Have you chosen one of these as your signature for now?

Why don't you circle it for me?

I love it. I really do. And guess what? I've discovered mine, too. It's a small stroke of purple. Why? Because purple is part blue and part red.

Red is passion and love. Blue is stability and trust.

So purple is when passion and love meet stability and trust.

And that is exactly what creation means to me.

Ha. That was some deep stuff right there. I should've been a poet.

What do you say we dip our fingers in paint and make our signatures again? And again? And then again?

See you the day after.

HAPPINESS AND...
THE WORLD

Date: / /   **Week 9: The World**

Hi there, Trickster.

I have a question for you today: Have you ever wondered what happiness means to the people around you? Yes? No? Maybe?

We are almost at the final leg of our journey together, bud. We have been at this for nine weeks now. But do you realize that we still haven't talked about what happiness actually means? To you? Or me? Heck, to the Oxford Dictionary?

Don't shake your head at me.

I told you right at the beginning: I'm not an expert on happiness. I'm just curious about it. I like thinking about it. And asking weird questions about it. And talking about it. A lot.

Would you like to do that too? Would you like to talk about happiness? And ask questions about it? Maybe even learn something new about it along the way?

YAY! This is going to be the absolute best.

So, listen closely now. Here's what I want you to do: Think of three different people that you would like to have these conversations with. Mix it up a little. Think of one tiny human. One adult human. And your favourite human. Done? Write down their names for me.

---

tiny human

---

adult human

---

favourite human

Now make a note of one question about happiness that you want to ask them. It can be as weird as you want. Like: What kind of flower sprouting out of their heads would make them the happiest? Or it can be as straightforward as you want. Like: What does happiness mean to them? Plain and simple.

Have you thought of one? Write it down here.

_____

_____

Ha! I love it. And now go and have these conversations. Right now. Just walk up to these humans. Or call them. Offer them some water. Or chocolate. And then sit down and remember to make them feel comfortable. Listen to them. Without any judgements. Without any interruptions. Even if you disagree with what they are saying. Or even if you think that you have a better answer than them. Or even if... You know what? It doesn't matter why. Just let them talk. And marvel at their answers like you would marvel at Nutella. All right?

Go on now. Have a few happy conversations. And jot down your favourite bits here. Ready? Go!

THIS IS WHAT I WILL REMEMBER FROM MY CONVERSATION WITH_____
(AKA TINY HUMAN)

Sigh. On to the next one…

THIS IS WHAT I WILL REMEMBER FROM MY CONVERSATION WITH _____
(AKA ADULT HUMAN)

And now the next…

THIS IS WHAT I WILL REMEMBER FROM MY CONVERSATION WITH_____
(AKA FAVOURITE HUMAN)

Now would you look at that? I love this. I really do.

Do you see, bud? Happiness means different things to different people. Heck, it may even mean different things to the same person at different points in time. Isn't that interesting?

Huh? What's that?

No, I don't know what you can do with this information. Why would I?

I was feeling left out and wanted to sound smart. That's all.

Psst! The Oxford Dictionary? It says happiness means the state of being happy. That's all.

Ha! Isn't that refreshingly simple?

Why don't you get out of here and think about what that means?

I'll see you tomorrow.

Hi there, Trickster.

I have something very simple in mind for you today.

Just spend some time with yourself.

Without any gadgets. Or to-do lists.

Without any need to hurry up.

And without anything else to distract you from you.

Spend a few minutes in complete solitude to check in with yourself. To have fun. To pay some attention to your heart. To your emotions. Your ideas. And your thoughts. Okay?

Think of it as taking yourself out on a playdate. Away from everything else. Just for a little while. Doesn't that sound nice?

You could do anything. You could take a walk through the park. Or write in a journal. Jump on a trampoline. Or dip your fingers in paint. Heck, you could just sit and breathe for five whole minutes if that's what you want. Because it doesn't matter what you do. As long as you are completely present with yourself while doing it.

Are you ready? Go on then. Take ten minutes off from your day. Spend them with yourself. And then come back to tell me how it went. I'll wait here. Maybe with some hot coffee and a chocolate donut?

There you are.

Welcome back, bud. Dig into the donut and tell me: What did you do? How did it go? And how do you feel right now?

I hear ya. I do.

Can I say something before you leave?

The thing is, pal: We live in a world that demands a lot of our time. That asks us to always be on the go. To always be doing something. Even when we are doing nothing. Do you know what I mean? And with all of our time that we are always giving away so freely to everyone else, isn't it possible for us to forget to stop and give at least some of it to ourselves too? Hm? I mean, think about it for a second: How much of your time is actually meant for you? And only you?

Na-uh. I'm not trying to get an answer out of you here, bud. All I'm trying to say is this: Remember to actively create some space for solitude in your life. Even if it feels uncomfortable. Especially if it feels uncomfortable.

Spend at least a few minutes alone every day. Schedule some time for yourself. Dang it, go ahead and put it on your calendar if you must. And while you're at it, take yourself out on a longer playdate every now and then, too. Take the chance to catch up with yourself. You are a very interesting person. And it will be worth your time. I can promise you that.

Don't worry about being unproductive on the playdate. Dunk your guilt in a cup of coffee that you enjoy with yourself every week. Do you hear me? Give your brain a moment to rest. To breathe. And do it often.

Now step away while I take myself out for a spin. Out of my way.

See you tomorrow.

Hi there, Trickster.

Would you like to hear a story?

Many years ago, on a warm Saturday afternoon, I had a conversation with a friend that changed my life. Or well, at least my perspective. Anyway, same difference, right?

I wasn't feeling all that great, so I asked them to meet me for a walk around the block. We talked about the trees for a few minutes. And then, I sat down on a bench and sighed. They picked up on it almost immediately and asked me if something wasn't right.

'Oh, I don't know,' I shrugged.

They turned towards me and said: 'Well, what if we figure it out together?'

That made me smile. So I nodded, ready to share my heart with them.

'I'm not feeling good about myself. You know? But it doesn't make any sense. I have been doing well at work. My friends are amazing. I get to see them as often I would like to. I'm busy doing all the things I enjoy doing and yet... Ugh, I don't know. I have just been so angry off late. For no good reason.'

'Congratulations!' they smiled.

'What? Did you not hear what I just said?' I asked, raising my eyebrow.

'Oh, I did. Maybe you did not hear what you just said?'

I looked at them all funny, silently daring them to say more.

'You say you are angry, right? That means you have your marching orders.'

That sounded like complete garbage to me. So naturally, I gave them the stink eye. They raised their hands and leaned forward.

'Look, all I'm trying to tell you is this: Anger is never bereft of meaning. I hear that you are uncomfortable, but if you'll just sit with that discomfort and work through it, maybe you will find that it actually makes sense. Maybe you will find that your anger holds a lot of wisdom within it. Don't roll your eyes at me. I mean it. If you think about it, anger is only a cue. It tells you when something isn't working for you. Then, it demands you pay attention to it and that you take steps to change it. Right away.'

...Whoa! That was all it took for my entire world to shift. I came back home that night and asked: 'Anger, buddy, is that you? What have you been trying to tell me for these past few weeks?'

And do you know what I realized? I realized that I wasn't nearly making as much time for myself as I would've liked to. My anger was telling me that I was stretching myself out too thin. It was telling me that I needed to pause. Rest. And reset.

Don't you see, bud? Anger was giving me my marching orders. It was directing me towards a life that would work better for me. That would be more fun for me. More fulfilling. Happier. Filled with more wonder. And more of the things that I truly cared about.

I guess what I'm saying is, even if your anger isn't as pleasant as hot tomato soup on a winter night, it is still worth paying attention to. You know? It may not be good. And it may not be bad. But it matters. Heck, it matters a lot. It gives you a whole lot of useful information.

So, stop shutting it up. And start acknowledging it, instead. Be curious about it. Ask questions from it. Allow it to slip you some intel when no one's looking. Let it tell you what you care about. What you need. Where you must establish boundaries. Talk to your anger, fam. And let it give you your marching orders. All right?

Pick up a pencil and make me a list of everything about the world that makes you angry. Think about the things that make your nerves tingle with frustration. That twist your stomach into big knots. The things that make you want to channel your inner Hulk. And just smash, you know? It could be some of the things that you read about in the papers. Or hear about on the radio. I mean, if they still have those around. Maybe you get angry when someone is being unkind. Or judgemental. Towards you. Or your friends. Your family. The trees. Or some puppies. Ugh. How can people be mean to puppies? Or... I don't know. It could be when you feel like you have no time left for yourself. Or for the things that you truly care about. Like building pillow forts. And looking at the stars. And jumping into water fountains. When you feel like you can't be yourself. And that you must keep wearing your masks. All the damn time. No matter how badly your fingers are cramping from holding them in place.

Do you have a few things popping up in your mind right now?

Why don't you jot them down here?

HULK ANGRY, HULK SMASH!

1. _____

2. _____

3. _____

4. _____

Ah, I see what you mean, buddy.

Now look at your list again. Stare at it for a few minutes. And ask: 'What information is my anger trying to give me here?'

Maybe it's telling you that you need to speak up. Or say no. Or that you need to take some time out for your hobbies. Because that piano isn't going to learn how to play itself. Or that there's some sort of a clash between your beliefs and actions. It could be anything, really.

You tell me. What is your anger telling you? What do your marching orders sound like?

I MUST MARCH TO THE TUNE OF...

1. _____
2. _____
3. _____
4. _____

Huh. Now would you look at that?

Who knew the big ol' scary red monster would actually know so much?

Remember this, champ. Remember to fish out intel from your emotions. Even the unpleasant ones. And if you have some trouble doing it yourself, holler. Ask for help. For assistance. For others to step in with their fishing rods. Just don't let the discomfort of experiencing an emotion stop you from communicating with it. All right?

Why don't you go think about this before you go to bed tonight?

And psst! Tell me: Do I always sound this smart?

Whaa? Fine. Just leave.

I'm going to have some tomato soup with bread and butter. Yum!

See you tomorrow.

Hi there, Trickster.

Can I ask you something?

Do you ever say yes when all you want is to say no? Yeah?

Ohmigosh! I thought I was the only one!

Eugh. Isn't it the worst? It is, isn't it?

Have you ever wondered why we do that, though? I mean, what makes us so scared of saying no? Of establishing boundaries? Of creating room for our preferences? Think about it: What makes us squirm and twist and wriggle our way out of uttering that one powerful word? Even if it costs us our time? Heck, even if it costs us our happiness?

Do you know what I'm talking about?

And let's just be terribly honest with each other for a second here: What bad and horrible things do we think will happen if we say no? What bad and horrible things have we concluded will happen if we say no?

Me? I'm scared that it'll be impolite. That it'll be rude. Or unkind. Or that I'll end up disappointing someone I care about. And hurt their feelings. Maybe even ruin their coffee. And be a very bad person. And… I don't know. Somehow cause the zombie apocalypse while I'm at it. You know?

What about you, bub? Tell me: What does saying no mean to you? What have you concluded will happen if you start saying no to the things you don't want to say yes to?

SAYING NO WILL BE THE ABSOLUTE WORST BECAUSE...

1. _____

2. _____

3. _____

4. _____

I get you, bud. I really, really do.

In fact, I have several of these same things on my list, too.

But here's the thing: Every single point on our lists? It's only a limitation that we have subscribed to. Do you see that? These are our fears. Our assumptions. Our ANTs. Our conclusions. And do you remember what we said about conclusions in the second week, champ? They lock us up. They make us small. And they leave us with no room for new possibilities. Or happiness. Remember that?

Do me a favour, bud? Dust off your toolbox. And use all the tricks you have learned so far. Use them so that you can step outside this particular box of limitations, too.

Look at each item on your list again. Take a moment to acknowledge how it is limiting you. Recognize that it's just a different point of view. And then replace it with a question, a suggestion or an idea, instead. And if the thought of uttering no still makes your stomach flip, then remember: Saying no to something will always mean saying yes to something else. Like yourself. Your time. And your happiness. So, tell yourself that you are allowed to say no. That you are allowed to be firm. Even when you are being kind. And gentle. And grateful, all right?

Give yourself permission to say no to the world when you want to.

And the permission to say yes to yourself every single time.

Now get out of here and practise saying no in front of the mirror. Go!

I'll see you tomorrow.

Hi there, Trickster.

Today is going to be a very interesting day. D'you know why? 'Cause today we are going to talk about every single good thing that we refuse to acknowledge about ourselves.

Oh, come on now. Don't start looking for escape routes just yet. I promise this isn't going to be some soppy old task where we sit down together and make a list of all that is good and bright and shiny about us.

Actually, on second thoughts… That's *exactly* what we should do! HA!

Glare at me later, will you? Just take a seat and hear me out already.

A couple of years ago, something strange would happen whenever somebody gave me a compliment. I would smile and nod and say all the right things, but… I don't know. Deep down, I was never really willing to receive the kindness in their words. And I wasn't ready to entertain the idea of someone in this world recognizing something good about me.

Let me tell you what happened once. I walked up on stage to give a talk at a book club. I stood straight, cleared my throat, opened with a funny joke, made some very good points and even did a somersault to close at the end. An actual somersault! Can you believe that?

You can?

Well, you shouldn't. Because it isn't exactly factually correct.

But that's not the point. The point is that I was good, all right?

Anyway, somebody found me when it was over and said: 'Congratulations, that was a lovely talk. The only way you could have topped that was if you had somersaulted your way off the stage!' And I did it again. I smiled graciously. Nodded humbly. Laughed along at all the right points. And thanked them for their kindness.

But guess what I was thinking the entire time? I was thinking that the only reason they said that to me was because they were sitting in the front row. And we had made eye contact. Twice. Then, I thought they were just feeling bad for me. Because I had paused for too long a second in the middle. And then I thought: 'Yeah, sure, I was okay, but what about the lady who spoke after me?

Now she was what I would call phenomenal...'

And so on and on and on...

Do you know what would have been a hundred times easier, bud? If I had just paused for a second to acknowledge and celebrate the fact that there was at least one person in the room who thought that I was amazing.

But, nope. Why would I ever consider doing that, right?

All the good and the bright and the shiny? I would only see it in others. Never in myself.

Tell me, bub: Have you ever done that too? Have you ever stopped yourself from truly receiving a compliment from somebody? Have you ever refused to acknowledge something that was good about yourself? Have you ever not celebrated yourself for something that the world was celebrating you for?

Well, while all of those scenarios make for excellent thought fodder at night, may I please suggest something a little bit different here?

What if you could begin to see the brilliance in yourself? With the utmost gratitude? And without any vanity? What if you could recognize all those great things about yourself that you have been ignoring forever? And what if you could gratefully accept all the kind words that the people around you have to say to you? Even when you think they are too good to be true?

Do that now, mate. Pick up a pencil and make me a list. Tell me about all of those great things that you haven't acknowledged in yourself yet. It could be how kind you really are. Or how much you care about birds and pandas and sunflowers. Or how amazing you are at air hockey. It could be anything. Anything at all.

LOOK! HERE'S ALL THAT IS GOOD AND BRIGHT AND SHINY IN ME

1. _____

2. _____

3. _____

4. _____

Whoa. Look at that. My eyes! You really know how to shine, don't you?

I think I'll go and make my list now, okay? See you tomorrow.

Hi there, Trickster.

Don't freak out when you hear this, but... I'm bored.

    Eugh. You heard me. I'm very, very bored.

    So, you will have to step in and entertain me today, okay?

    Hmm... Let me see... Oh, I know! Get us out of here. Right now. Step out into the open and look at the streets. Or the skies. Or the trees. Take a few moments to observe the world around you. And notice four interesting things that are happening out there.

    Come on. Get at it.

    ...Are you done? Why don't you write them down here?

THIS IS WHAT I NOTICED ON THE STREETS TODAY

1. _____

2. _____

3. _____

4. _____

Oh. More?

5. _____

6. _____

7. _____

Well, what do you know? Nicely noticed, Sherlock.

    Now pick item #3 from your list. And write me a funny story around it. I don't know how. You've done it before. You'll do it again. Go on. Bring in the funny. Entertain me.

HAHAHAHAHA. Stop, stop, stop! My tummy hurts.

And gosh. Who knew there were so many interesting things in the world to keep an eye out for, amirite? Huh. Maybe we should remember that.

I'm going to go put your story up on the Internet now, okay? I mean, why should I be the only one who's laughing?

See you the day after.

HAPPINESS AND...
SOME REFLECTION

Date: / /   **Week 10: Some Reflection**

Hi there, Trickster.

There you are. Can you believe we made it this far?

Gosh. Thanks for sticking around, buddy. You're a champ. Well, so am I, but let's keep this about you, yeah?

Tell me something: Were there any moments along this journey when you didn't feel like coming back to me? Hm? It's all right, pal. It really is. I understand. In fact, to tell you the truth, I expected it.

Because you see, I have been there, too. I have begun projects and adventures with all my heart. And then wished I never had. I have had days and days of moping around and wondering why I even said yes to something in the first place.

But d'you know why I kept moving forward? I mean, apart from the very obvious reason that I'm awesome? I kept moving forward because I was committed. To the idea. To the journey. Heck, most of all, to myself. And I had an inkling that if I just kept at it, then all of the different phases would eventually fade away. And tell you what? They did.

When I kept showing up—day after day—my will did, too.

Do you see where I'm going with this?

Commitment is indispensable to any trickster's journey, mate. It is an essential thing for us to cultivate in our lives. For us to practise. With great intention. And that is exactly what I want us to do today.

I'm going to bring out a fancy scroll. And you are going to write down some vows on it. Vows of happy living. And of keeping at it. No matter what.

I mean, it's like they say: You didn't come this far to only come this far, right?

Hm, what else? I'm not going to tell you about all the different kinds of promises that you can make here, bud. I'm only going to ask you to fill it with as much wonder and joy as you possibly can, okay?

If this journey were a friend you were making some promises to, what would these promises be? To pay attention to it? To spend some time with it? And to always come back to it? What promises are you making today? Why don't you write them down?

Wow. Look at that.

What do you say we fold it up real tight in a glass bottle and set it afloat at sea? No? Ugh. Where's your sense of drama?

Fine. Just cut it out and keep it under your pillow, instead.

Psst: Can I say something before you leave?

This was the final step you needed to take to become a certified trickster. Along with everything else, I meant for this to become a hallmark of the journey that we have taken together.

Which led us to this point.

Where I step out.

And the vows step in.

What a ride, bud. What a ride.

Damn it. I can feel a speech rising at the back of my throat. But it will have to wait for a while. Because I have something to show you right now. Look!

It's your very own trickster crown!

Yes, it's a little rusty. No, those pearls aren't real.

And no, you definitely cannot ask people to curtsy in front of you.

I mean, what even... Just why?

But that's not the point, is it? The point is that you get to wear this crown whenever you would like to. You get to be a trickster whenever you would like to. You have all the tools, spells and epiphanies that you need. You are ready.

Leap forward towards new adventures, my friend. Trust that the winds will carry you. And find your gravity in this flight. Sounds good? Good.

Now off you fly, free bird.

See you tomorrow.

Hi there, Trickster.

Is this really happening?
 Ohmigosh! Why is this happening? Our time together is almost up!
 Yikes. I have a whole lot of feelings right now.
 But this isn't about me. Not right now, at least.
 We have spent the last ten weeks learning how to become tricksters together. We have walked a long, long way. We have asked questions. Cheered each other on. Painted skies. Stepped out of boxes. We have had some fun, haven't we?
 Tell me, bub: What are you thinking of right now? What are you feeling? A sense of accomplishment? Some nostalgia? Relief? Contentment? Or some bittersweet emotions you don't quite know how to name?

Thanks for sharing that with me, you. I like listening to you. You are an amazing person, aren't you?
 See you tomorrow.

Hi there, Trickster.

Is it a Thursday today? 'Cause I'm about to roll a throwback!

What? Why are you laughing? Did I not pull that off okay? But I have been practising all night! Eugh. Whatever. I don't care much for these stupid Internet trends, anyway.

Now would you please stop laughing and do as I say?

Do you remember seeing this before?

Yeah? We called it the Ladder of Self-Confidence.

Is it still upside down? And a teensy bit crooked now, too?

Eh, I bet it still works fine.

What I have in mind for you today is fairly simple. All I want you to do is to look at the ladder again and tell me which rung you are standing on right now. You have done this before. You can do it again. Trust your gut. And know that you already know.

Look at the ladder and tell me, bud: Where are you standing at this very moment? Is it the same step you were on in the seventh week? Or have you moved a little further along? You could, at this moment, be standing at a lower rung, too. And that's okay. It's all okay. There are no right or wrong answers here. You know that by now, don't you?

_____

_____

Okay. That's cool.

And now, just like the last time, why don't you make me a list of all the barriers that are stopping you from going just one step higher?

WHAT'S STOPPING ME FROM GOING HIGHER ON
THE LADDER OF SELF-CONFIDENCE?

1. _____

2. _____

3. _____

4. _____

I hear ya. And finally, tell me: Are there any tools currently available to you that you can use to get rid of these barriers?

WOULD YOU LOOK AT MY COOL TOYS? I MEAN TOOLS.

1. _____

2. _____

3. _____

4. _____

I see. That's all I wanted to know.

Will you do me a favour, bud? Will you keep checking in here every six months? To ask yourself where you are standing on the Ladder of Self-Confidence? To identify all the barriers that are keeping you there? And then to use the tools you have to go just one step higher? Yeah?

You can go now.

Wait! Just tell me one more thing.

Do you not roll a throwback? Was that it? Do you spin it, instead?

Oh, for goodness' sake. STOP LAUGHING. I'll figure it out myself.

See you tomorrow.

Hi there, Trickster.

Do you know what eureka means? Such a wonderful little word, isn't it?

Eureka. I've found it. That's literally what it means.

I don't know if you have heard of this story in a science class already, but it's said that Archimedes, the Greek scientist, once ran out on the streets shouting 'Eureka!' at the top of his voice after he discovered a way to calculate density and volume while sitting in his bathtub. You heard me. In his bathtub! Isn't that crazy?

Eureka is the moment you find something. It is unexpected. Sudden. And in most cases, deeply inspiring. I have had quite a few of those moments in the past ten weeks. How could I not? I learned how to judge a little less. I realized that most of my fears aren't even mine. I met my bluebird. Used my voice. Practised how to say yes. And no. I went on grand adventures with you every single week. I mean, really, how could I not?

Have you had any such moments too, bud? In the last ten weeks, have you discovered anything new? Or remembered something you hadn't realized you had forgotten? About yourself? Or the world? Have you had any unexpected and inspiring moments of sudden realisation? Why don't you make me a list?

EUREKA! EUREKA! EUREKA!

1. _____
2. _____
3. _____
4. _____

Wow. Would you look at that? You have had quite a few epiphanies, haven't you? Are you secretly a very smart person? I'm kidding, I'm kidding! Gosh! Shouldn't you know better by now? Get out of here and study density and volume. Out! I'll see you tomorrow.

Hi there, Trickster.

I just finished looking over the list you made last night. And it was spectacular. Isn't it cool to think how much we can learn about ourselves just by spending a few minutes in our own company every day?

Can I be honest? That's all that I have tried to get you to do up until now. I mean, I know I have been there with you, too. But all I have done is ask you a few questions. And then given you some time with yourself to think about them. All of my prompts were meant for you to be truly present with yourself. Even if it was only for fifteen minutes a day.

Do you think you will still keep that going after we are done here tomorrow? In fact, tell me this: Is there anything from our journey that you would like to include in your daily life? A tool? A thought? Your way of being?

Maybe you would like to remember to disarm a judgement by calling it a different point of view. Maybe you would like to redo your permission slip every New Year's Eve. Maybe you would like to keep on using affirmations and gratitude to squash your ANTs. And maybe you would like to ask yourself lots of questions, step outside a lot of assumptions and go on lots of fun adventures. And maybe… You would like to come back to visit me every now and then, too.

Can you think of anything at all?

Pick up your pencil and make yourself a list, bud.

List all the things that you would like to continue doing from tomorrow. Write it all down now so that you don't forget. And feel free to flip through the pages if you can't quite remember that one thing you enjoyed doing very much.

THIS LIST WILL MAKE ME CRY BUT HERE GOES ANYWAY

1. _____

2. _____

3. _____

4. _____

Have you run out of space? Create more of it then. Create as much of it as you need.

And now, tie a thread here so that you can remember to check in on this page every once in a while. And you know, feel free to say hello to me while you're at it.

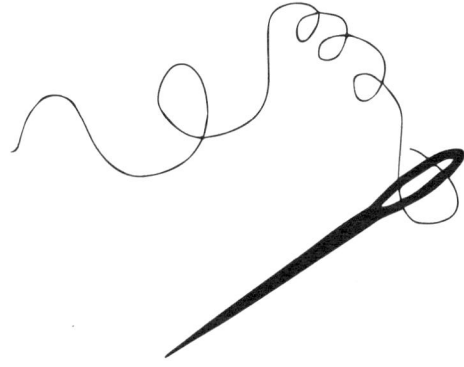

Damn it. I'm getting all teary.

You better leave. This isn't going to be pretty.

GOOOOO!

See you tomorrow.

Hi there, Trickster.

Can I talk to you about change today?

You see, after you left last night, I began thinking about our time together. And I realized I'm not the same book that I was when we had first started out.

I have changed. And thank goodness for that.

You see bud, for the most part, I don't think change is bad. It's necessary. It can be beautiful. And it can create room for new possibilities in your life. For new adventures. Creation. Vulnerability. And growth.

I'm not the book that I was. And I'm not the book that I will be. I have changed. And the one thing that I can count on? I will change again. You will change again. I find a strange kind of comfort in that fact. Do you?

Stay with that thought and write a letter. Write a letter to yourself that you will read a year from now. Be present with the knowledge that you will have changed. In ways that you can't possibly begin to imagine right now.

Is there anything that you would like to say to your future self? Is there anything that you would like to remind them of? It could be some epiphany that you have stumbled upon in the last ten weeks. Or it could be a very funny joke that you read on the Internet earlier this morning. You could even nudge your future self to paint with their fingers every now and then. And to keep breathing whenever things get a little tough.

Write a letter to your future self. Go all out. Say all that you need to. Say all that you would like to. Grab your pencil. And just begin.

Don't think too much, bub.

Show up at the page.

And maybe the words will, too.

Sigh. My heart. Now come back to this page 365 days later as a new person. Change, after all, has a way of sneaking up on us.

Psst: Don't feel like you can't come visit sooner though, okay? You can pop in and say hi whenever you would like to. Just don't read this letter when you do, all right?

Cool. Well, I guess this is it then, buddy. Off you go now. Onto new adventures. Is there anything that you would like to say to me before you leave?

I hear you. Can I say something now, too? I have had the time of my life with you in these ten weeks, champ. And I am really going to miss hanging out with you. Very, very much.

Where do we go from here now? Onwards. Upwards. Inwards.

Carry whatever you would like to from this journey along with you and move forward. Walk towards new adventures with memories of this one. Pack light. Have gratitude. Use your voice. And your imagination. Show up. Be fierce. And flawed. Dance. Keep breathing. Let the world enchant you with beauty. Marvel. And remember to check your teeth for lettuce before you walk inside a room, okay?

Time for you to leave now, pal. But did you really think I was going to let you go anywhere without a present? Ha! Close your eyes. Don't look!

Okay, I'm ready. Are you?

Aren't they absolutely and unbelievably adorable? Plant friends are the best.

They remind you to keep it simple. To slow down. And to drink lots of water. Take good care of 'em, okay? I'm going to pop in for some random investigations.

Out with you now. See you to… Oh. Right. I'll see you when I see you.

A WORD BEFORE YOU LEAVE

Hi there, you.

Or do you prefer being called a Trickster? Welcome to the other side of the journey! I heard you've had quite the ride. And I'm glad to see you made it here without any scratches. Or bumps on your head. Or spinach in your teeth. Before you leave, I have a couple of things to tell you. First, because I think you're kinda awesome, I have a gift for you: two additional free (unpublished) chapters of this book. HA! Isn't that awesome? So, if you'd like to continue on the journey you began here, go on the Internet and visit www.simranbhui.com. I'll tell you what to do once you get there, okay?

And second, I wanted to let you know what to expect when you flip this page. You see, I have always dreamt of taking the stage at the Grammys. Ever since I was a little girl. Quite obviously, that hasn't happened yet, so I'm going to play pretend and give a long-winded acceptance speech on the next page. It took me hours to write, so I expect you to stick with me till the very last word. Which is 'over' in case you were wondering. Ahem, ahem. Here I go...

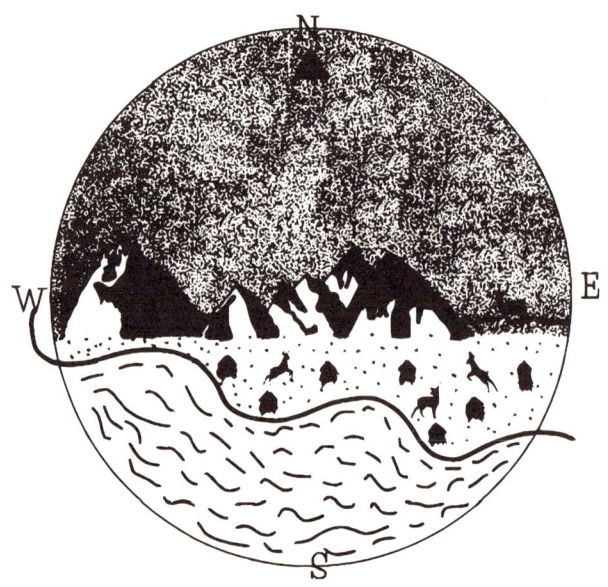

Let the world enchant you with beauty.

ACKNOWLEDGEMENTS

My unbridled joy and gratitude to my parents, Manjit Singh and Balvinder Kaur, for being my gravity and flight; to Sujay Suresh for talking me down from every ledge in my head and encouraging me to create more room for myself in life; to Guneet Khurana, Manvir Singh, Iqbal Kaur and Gurdev Khurana for celebrating every small victory by bringing me the yummiest food; to every child (Gyaan, Gagan, Kiaan...) who taught me the meaning of happy living; to Amrisha Ahuja and Guninder Bhui for reminding me to slow down and keep it simple; to Vineet Kaur for the 3 a.m. epiphany that turned into this book; to Ashmit Bhui and Jasmine Bindra for always giving my ideas a physical form; to Surmit Bhui for being the most wonderful sounding board a sister could ask for (all while building satellites that are orbiting the Earth as we speak); to Pia Bakshi for helping me find my bluebird; to Kiran Singh and Rattan Deep Singh for being the kindest people I've ever known; to Mridula Sridhar, Ramya Venkataraman and Kanika Parwal for believing in this project and taking it to the streets; to Blossom Benedict—if magic could speak, its words would echo hers; to Elizabeth Gilbert for *Big Magic*; and to all of my friends, mentors and teachers for encouraging me to create fiercely over the last few years.

As it often happens whenever I try to sketch something, zombies threatened to take over the world. Guneet, Sujay and Pia: You were my lifelines. Thank you for saving the world with your sharpened pencils and brand new sketchbooks. These pages speak of your generosity. This book would also not have existed if it weren't for the exceedingly talented team at Rupa. Thank you for holding my words with care.

A big shout-out to my brother, Manvir, for never failing to remind me of my chosen purpose (even if it meant hitting me over the head with a bat. Okay, maybe not an actual bat). This one's for you.

For much of my life, my mind has been racing to keep up with my heart. To everyone who has honoured my choices, made space for them and cheered me on while I went on new adventures, thank you a million times over.

—S

Are you ready for a new adventure?